DATE DUE

MAY 18 1969		
APR 4 1986		
FEB 2 1988		

LINCOLN IMAGES

CARL SANDBURG
A son of Swedish immigrants and a Lincoln scholar

LINCOLN IMAGES

Augustana College Centennial Essays

by

O. FRITIOF ANDER, ERNEST M. ESPELIE

NORMAN A. GRAEBNER, RALPH J. ROSKE

ROBERT M. SUTTON, CLYDE C. WALTON

T. HARRY WILLIAMS

Edited by

O. FRITIOF ANDER

AUGUSTANA COLLEGE LIBRARY

ROCK ISLAND, ILLINOIS

1960

AUGUSTANA LIBRARY PUBLICATIONS
No. 29

ERNEST M. ESPELIE, *General Editor*

Library of Congress Card Number 60-12543

⟦PRINTED
IN U·S·A⟧

AUGUSTANA BOOK CONCERN
Printers and Binders
ROCK ISLAND, ILLINOIS

Dedicated

to

Carl Sandburg

A Son of Swedish

Immigration

Foreword

AUGUSTANA COLLEGE AND THEOLOGICAL SEMINARY were the noblest and most ambitious ventures of the Swedish immigrants who began to come in great numbers to this country a century ago. The Augustana Centennial recalls the memory of these people, and especially of those who dared dream dreams and see visions above the paucity of their belongings and the preoccupation of the daily task.

Among the Swedish community in Illinois were the parents of Carl Sandburg, and the first pastor of their church in Galesburg had become president of Augustana College, a post he held for a quarter of a century. As editor, too, of the first and most widely read newspaper in the immigrant homes, T. N. Hasselquist wielded a tremendous influence. An ardent champion of Abraham Lincoln he probably did more than any other one individual to create the Lincoln image which became implanted in the minds of the Swedish folk in America.

In dedicating these essays to Carl Sandburg, the authors express their admiration for one of the foremost of the children of the immigration. They pay a tribute of gratitude, also, to the men and women of the old world who followed inspired leadership as they sought to create a new world where freedom and righteousness might be the lot of every citizen.

Augustana College counts it a privilege to sponsor this publication as a part of its centennial in 1960.

CONRAD BERGENDOFF

Rock Island, Illinois

Founders' Day, April 27, 1960

vii

Contents

Introduction

The founders of Augustana College were contemporaries of Abraham Lincoln. Lars P. Esbjörn was born in 1808 a year earlier than Lincoln while T. N. Hasselquist was born six years later. The scope of the study of immigration has expanded to include not only the westward movement in the United States but ideas, institutions, and customs which transcend barriers. The impulses which brought Lincoln, born in Kentucky, to Illinois are not unrelated to those forces which impelled Esbjörn and Hasselquist to immigrate to Illinois. Whether people emigrated from New England, the Middle Atlantic States, the South or Europe, they sought as far as possible to reestablish the old community which they had left. Names of towns and cities in Illinois and other states testify to the dreams of their founders. When a group of Scandinavian immigrants established Augustana College, which for a time was situated in Chicago, they too were striving to reestablish in the New World a part of the old community. It was incidental that Lincoln had been nominated as the presidential candidate at the Republican National Convention in Chicago and that he triumphed at the polls two months after Augustana College had opened the doors to its first students. Lincoln was, however, no stranger to the founders of the college.

The college evolved from Illinois State University, maintained by the Synod of Northern Illinois, situated in Springfield. Lincoln, who had established a perpetual scholarship at the university in 1852, which his son Robert Todd used, was elected a member of its Board of Trustees in 1860. In the same year the founders of Augustana College were the staunchest supporters of Lincoln and the Republican party and they played a part, even though perhaps small, in his election to the presidency.

It, therefore, seemed proper that Augustana College should in 1960 publish *Lincoln Images: Augustana College Centennial Essays* honoring both Lincoln and the founders of Augustana College.

Wendell H. Stephenson in "A quarter century of American historiography," *Mississippi Valley Historical Review,* June, 1958, expressed a concern over the growth and nature of the literature on Lincoln and the Civil War. The approach of the centennial of Lincoln's election in 1860, the Civil War, and Lincoln's martyr death of 1865 will further swell this literature. Perhaps Carl Sandburg's *Prairie Years,* written in a "Carlylesque technique" or a true Sandburg-story-telling style, launched the revolution while Stephen Benet's *John Brown's Body* further whetted the public's appetite. Historians, journalists, and novelists stimulated by an inspiring theme fanned the fervor of the Lincoln cult. It is understandable that in such a flood of literature there are many "thrice-told-tales" and little which is characterized by historical objectivity. Perhaps a best seller of today might be labeled *Rendezvous with Rover: Lincoln's Wife's Doctor's Dog.* In the midst of this trivia it is refreshing to be able to turn to such significant works as those of Carl Sandburg, James G. Randall, T. Harry Williams, Paul M. Angle, Benjamin P. Thomas, Harry E. Pratt, Jay Monaghan, David Donald, Bell Wiley, Bruce Catton, William B. Hesseltine, Douglas Freeman, Avery Craven, Roy Nichols, Frank Vandiver, Allan Nevins and others.

It is hoped that *Lincoln Images* dedicated to Sandburg and written by friends and students of Randall might reflect credit on the craftsmanship and scholarship of both these great Lincoln scholars. T. Harry Williams is an heir to Randall's fame as a student of Lincoln. He possesses "the tolerant, human understanding and insight" which Stephenson saw in Randall. The fact that he is born in Illinois, received his Ph.D. at the University of Wisconsin, and has taught for several years in the South might have influenced his depth of understanding of both the North and the South.

Norman A. Graebner edited *The Enduring Lincoln,* to which volume Williams contributed an essay. Graebner's major field of interest is, however, the diplomatic history of the United States. Like Williams he is known not only as a scholar but a popular lecturer and teacher, and the present critical international situation might have prompted him to write on the realistic policy of national interest pursued by Lincoln. Students of Lincoln are able to look forward to a forthcoming volume of Graebner's in the Chicago History of American Civilization series entitled, *The Troubled Union, 1837-1865*.

Robert M. Sutton, a colleague of Graebner's at the University of Illinois, reflects the influence of both Randall and Theodore C. Pease with whom he studied. Although he has followed more in the footsteps of the latter than the former he has a genuine interest in the life of Lincoln and particularly its Illinois foundations. Sutton is an authority on the history of Illinois and the Illinois Central Railroad.

Ralph J. Roske of Humboldt State College is also a product of Randall, who directed Roske's interest in Lyman Trumbull. An important study of Trumbull is long overdue and Roske's essay is a significant contribution. Roske is the co-author of *Lincoln's Commando*.

Clyde C. Walton and Ernest Espelie are librarians with a deep appreciation of history. Walton succeeded such Lincoln scholars as Angle, Monaghan, and Pratt to the position which he now holds. He learned to know and value Randall both as a friend and a scholar. Watlon has, therefore, centered his essay on Randall's well known article "Has the Lincoln theme been exhausted?" which appeared in the *American Historical Review*, January, 1936.

The librarian of the Denkmann Memorial Library of Augustana College, Ernest Espelie, has provided for *Lincoln Images* an interesting bibliography of Lincoln books and pamphlets found at Augustana College. Although the number of titles might not seem large when one considers that about 5,000 books have been written about Lincoln, the titles in the bibliography are of interest when it is known that no effort has been made by the college to build a Lincoln library. Many of Espelie's references consist of several volumes.

Like most of the contributors, the editor of *Lincoln Images* was also a friend and student of Randall. He was a student, too, of Marcus Lee Hansen and his chief interest has been the history of immigration.

Carl Sandburg is a son of the Swedish immigration which founded Augustana College. The contributors of these essays believe that dedicating these essays to Sandburg is a fitting tribute to him and to the founders of Augustana College.

O. FRITIOF ANDER

xiii

O. FRITIOF ANDER

Lincoln and

The Founders of Augustana College

The Almighty has his own purposes. "Woe unto the world because of offenses! for it must needs be that offenses come; but woe to that man by whom the offense cometh." (From Lincoln's Second Inaugural Address)

The spring which gave the Republican party Abraham Lincoln as its candidate for the presidency of the United States had given birth to a less heralded event, the Evangelical Lutheran Augustana Synod of North America. The harvest season brought its fruits. Augustana College and Seminary opened its doors in the city which had seen Lincoln nominated. Later Lincoln triumphed at the polls.

Swedish immigrants, like other immigrants, wished to experience a new birth by renouncing old world loyalties and accepting democratic faiths so that they might share American sorrows and joys. Thus they hoped to possess and be possessed, to love and be loved. The tempestuous decade of the 50's sparked the rebirth, and the Civil War offered a sacrament of blood.

In the process of Americanization enter ingredients which to the brilliant Henry Adams might have seemed senseless as to sequence of man, society, time, and thought. Yet, Adams pondered seriously upon what "turned the European peasant into a new man within half an hour after landing in New York?" The answer was certainly to be found in the challenge of liberty and the abundance of opportunities which caused the immigrant to see visions of mountains of salt, iron, lead, copper, silver, and gold to be mined; forests to be felled, and virgin soil to be tilled.

Although the immigrants were influenced by these visions, hidden even to poets, many of them did not shed their sacred religious beliefs. The founding of the Augustana Lutheran Church and that of Augustana

1

College and Theological Seminary are illustrations of determined hopes of immigrants to preserve and transplant on American soil creeds and rituals hallowed by European experiences. The immigrants claimed for themselves in 1860 the right of freedom of worship still denied to many Europeans. It is understandable that they felt drawn closer to God in their native language. It made them feel at home in the "New Zion." Through it they interpreted the scriptures of the American way of life. But it stamped them as foreigners, and as a result they turned to politics to claim for themselves the most cherished of American liberties—the right to vote.

It is not possible to overestimate the impact of a series of events on the political horizon which charged the decade of the 50's with excitement that culminated in a tense national interest in the election of 1860. Perhaps it was a coincidence that a group of immigrants, who in 1851 had affiliated with the Synod of Northern Illinois, established an ethnic church, college, and seminary in the very year that they rallied to support Lincoln.

Henry Adams thought that the most difficult historical problem of all was the study of the national character in the absence of a formula which would explain the role of popular imagination. Nationalism craves faiths in which symbols, heroes, and adversaries play an important role. Many of these were brought by immigrants, facilitating the process of Americanization. Thus, the mighty armies of Gustavus Adolphus were enrolled anew as battle lines formed around Abraham Lincoln, who became the mighty lion of the North, the David of old who slew Goliath and drove the Philistines into flight, and the redeemer President. When the voice of Jehovah was heard in the sound of cannons as the children of Israel fought the offender through whom the offenses had come, the people had claimed the country and the country, the immigrants.

The founders of the Augustana Lutheran Church were engaged in the task of preserving a part of the Old World in America while at the same time they sought to assist the immigrants in discovering the deeper significance of our democratic doctrines. The challenge was great. Most immigrants had lost the faith of their fathers before they left Europe. To these nationalism became a surrogate for Christianity, while Methodists,

2

Baptists, and Lutherans waged war upon the ancient foe, the devil, without agreeing upon a frontal attack, obedient to only one common loyalty, America. By 1860 the spires of the Swedish Lutheran immigrant churches were decked by American flags, hiding partly the cross and dulling the sound of bells. The process of Americanization was complete except for creeds and language. It was, therefore, important that these be preserved as a significant heritage of and link with Europe. This was the task of the little remnant.

Lars P. Esbjörn, T. N. Hasselquist, Erland Carlsson, O. C. T. Andreen, and Jonas Swensson were educated at the universities of Sweden and ordained into the ministry of the Established Church of Sweden. When "America fever" began to spread causing many sons of the soil to emigrate, these men of God, touched by a religious awakening, joined them to save the little remnant. They lost themselves in their cause and they became the remnant. They were all different; they were individualists, drawn together by a common mission and held together by forces which they could not control.

It was Esbjörn who arrived first. The immigrants were poor and scattered. Esbjörn received financial support from the American Home Missionary Society without feeling that he had compromised his religious beliefs. Desperately lonely he sought the fellowship and comfort of native American Lutherans who formed the Synod of Northern Illinois.

Hasselquist, Carlsson, and others arrived, but their numbers were inadequate. Hasselquist established a Swedish-American newspaper, *Hemlandet, Det Gamla och Det Nya,* (The Old and the New Homeland) in order to keep intact the ties of the immigrants. The little remnant found it necessary to co-operate with the Synod of Northern Illinois in supporting the Illinois State University, where a Scandinavian chair could be established and men trained for ministering to the spiritual needs of the immigrants. But funds were required and someone to fill the chair. Finally Esbjörn, who succeeded in securing financial support from American Lutherans of the Atlantic seaboard states, was selected as the Scandinavian professor.

The immigrants were caught in both centripetal and centrifugal forces. Necessity compelled them to turn to native American Lutherans for assistance while the desire for the preservation of their ethnic entity bred discord and disunity. The era of good feeling in America had faded away. It had left its marks, including the General Synod, a co-operative effort of a group of Lutherans of which the Synod of Northern Illinois was a part. Forms and rituals had been modified and less stress was placed upon creeds and confessions. In many Protestant churches the "Swallow's nest" had disappeared and its place was taken by a lectern and a platform permitting clergymen to express their feelings and sentiments in fuming, gesticulating, orating, damning the black sheep, cheering the weary, and praising the faithful. The romantic religion of the Savior was no less popular in well established communities than on the frontier. But many of those brought up in old churchly traditions of Europe found the orating parson distasteful in manner and shameless in unorthodoxy.

The immigrants came from many parts of Europe. No church of the Reformation had suffered more from territorialism than the Lutheran. Its disunity was complete; it transcended ethnic and linguistic barriers; yet each Lutheran body believed itself to be the true child of the father of the Reformation. When immigrants protested against American religious tolerance and the excessive sentimentalism of romantic Christianity, they spoke in many tongues and no one understood the other. They had also settled in many regions of America. To the distrust bred by European territorialism was added American environmentalism, which was no less divisive. Thus, the effort on the part of a small group of Scandinavians to co-operate with some American Lutherans in supporting the Illinois State University was doomed to fail. The centrifugal forces were greater than the centripetal. But the attempt was not without historical significance in the Americanization of the founders of the Augustana Lutheran Church and Augustana College. They learned to like and respect Americans, with perhaps a small appreciation of their religious tolerance.

The Swedes learned to know Lincoln through their association with the Illinois State University at Springfield, as well as through the pages of *Hemlandet,* and active participation in the elections of 1858 and 1860. By 1861 they were ready to answer his call to arms.

John T. Stuart, Lincoln's first law partner, had played a greater role than anyone else in inducing Hillsboro College to move to Springfield in 1852 where the new institution was hopefully given the impressive and aspiring name, Illinois State University. Stuart, together with a group of public spirited citizens of Springfield, including Abraham Lincoln, had subscribed $37,000.00 for a building and scholarship fund.

Stuart had expressed his hopes for the university in a letter to Dr. S. W. Harkey in the following words: "No institution in the West, within my knowledge, has commenced with so much means, to say nothing of the good wishes and united sentiments of the wealthy community in whose midst it will be planted." The first president of the university, Francis Springer, a descendant of the Swedish colonists of Delaware, hoped that the university would become a center of Christian learning which would have a leavening effect upon American ecclesiasticism and evangelization of the immigrants bearing the Lutheran name.

But the university was to be constantly plagued by financial difficulties. Money subscribed was not easily collected. Misfortune and misunderstanding followed. The university became the battlefield of New Lutheranism represented by Francis Springer and Old Lutheranism identified by Lars P. Esbjörn. The former received the support of most native Lutherans while Esbjörn was the spokesman for the Scandinavians. Unfortunately the scope of the Scandinavian professorship had not been defined. The American influences at Springfield were stronger than those of the immigrants. The latter had only five representatives on the Board of Trustees of the university, while twenty-six were native born. The charter of the institution, drafted by Francis Springer, stipulated that one-third of the trustees were to be selected from among citizens of Springfield and vicinity. Springer was a nativist who was "a fearless pleader for the ascendancy of Americans in America" in matters pertaining to the church, state, science, literature, and "everything else." He expected the immigrants in America to be Americans. He resented efforts by them to obtrude "cumbrous churchliness" of Europe upon "the new and nobler nationality to which they had fled." In fact, in the original charter Springer did not state that Lutherans had an exclusive right to govern the policies of the university. He wished to escape every appearance of sectarianism. When S. W. Harkey became professor of theology at Springfield he sought the favor of the immigrants and succeeded in amending the charter allow-ing the Lutheran bodies which supported it to elect two-thirds of the Board of Trustees. He also placed a stricter confessional obligation upon himself and exalted "Lutheranism," thus seeking to combine the orthodox among American Lutherans and the immigrants. Harkey made Springer's position as president impossible and for a time Harkey was named tem-porary president. But the Lutherans of Illinois continued to drift apart, Springer taunted the immigrants that formalism would cause spiritual death and his dislike for Harkey grew bitter when he himself and his followers were labeled "little theologians" and "Methodists," "brethren weak in the faith." In fact by 1859 Springer believed that the university had fallen into the hands of the Europeans of the Synod of Northern Illinois with their hyperorthodoxy and symbolism. He desired, therefore, that American Lutherans withdraw and form a new synod to be called the English Lutheran Synod of Illinois.

Letters written by Springer to alienate the English-speaking Lutherans toward the university were published late in 1859 and early in 1860 in the *Olive Branch*. S. W. Harkey meanwhile urged "continued unity" as the doctrinal basis of the General Synod, a policy which did not please the Scandinavians. Thus, the meetings of the Synod of Northern Illinois became more and more strained.

Harkey during his short tenure as president of Illinois State Univer-sity had mortgaged his home in Maryland to assist the university to meet some of its obligations. He insisted on payment, but he had to settle for a library of 1,200 volumes, twelve recitation benches, thirty seats, and a color microscope in return for $3,000.00 he had lent the university. He was also demoted to professor while Dr. W. M. Reynolds was made president. Reynolds, a clergyman from Pennsylvania, found his task as Springer's successor more and more difficult. He sought to make peace where there was no peace. Meanwhile the university was unable to pay the salaries of its professors. The Panic of 1857 had made collections of scholarship pledges nearly impossible.

During these trying times, it is difficult to say what interest Lincoln might have taken in the university. Lincoln, who was a law partner of Wm. H. Herndon when Illinois State University was founded, had bought

6

a "perpetual scholarship" for the sum of $300.00 in the original drive to secure the university for Springfield. The owner of such a scholarship had the right to send one student to the college without payment of tuition. Such a scholarship could be maintained by payments of an annual interest of six per cent. Lincoln used this type of scholarship in sending his son, Robert Todd, to school. It was purchased on October 1, 1852, and Lincoln continued to pay interest rates on it regularly until April 27, 1860. The interest amounted to $19.50 a year. Besides, Lincoln was asked to pay an annual incidental fee of $1.50. The registrar's records of the university listed Lincoln as "a responsible person," and in 1858 "honorable" was added to his title, a title given earlier to many persons less known than Lincoln.

Robert Todd enrolled in the preparatory department in the fall of 1853 at the age of eleven; he was one of the youngest students. By attending summer school he was permitted to enter the college as a freshman at the age of thirteen. He was not a genius. His grades were average except in declamation and composition where he received grades of 60. He had to take an oath not to use profane language, gamble, or resist authority. In 1856 he became a member of the Philomathean Society, but he lacked interest in it and was once fined for failing to attend its meetings. He was made recording secretary the year that his father debated Douglas, but having attended only two meetings he requested an honorable dismissal. Although he did not attend any more meetings of the society he was prevailed upon to withdraw his resignation. In the fall of the same year Robert Todd left the university to continue his studies at Phillips Academy.

There are good reasons to believe that Robert Todd was unhappy at the university. This might have been a factor in Lincoln's refusal to accept honorary membership in the Philomathean Society, which was offered him on two occasions. Almost every person of note in Springfield was an honorary member of one of the two literary societies. Many national figures of importance were happy to express their pleasure of being thus honored. The Philomathean Society became in 1858 a pro-Lincoln society while its rival the Utilior Society was pro-Douglas. The little giant frequently contributed gifts to the library of the Utilior Society, but

Lincoln remained aloof from the Philomathean Society. During the year 1858-1859 the Lincoln scholarship was used by Lincoln Dubois, a son of Jessie K. Dubois.

Robert Todd Lincoln was not the only one who was unhappy at Illinois State University. The Utilior Society had again and again expressed anti-Scandinavian sentiments. It had seriously considered the motion that no membership in the society should be granted to a person who was not able to express himself clearly in English. Lars P. Esbjörn, who had accepted the Scandinavian professorship, was never happy in Springfield. His reaction to Springfield might well have been similar to that of John Hay's first impression when he enrolled at the university in 1853. Hay wrote: "I am stranded at last, like a weather-beaten hulk, on the dreary wastes of Springfield—a city combining the meanness of the North with the barbarism of the South." Or Esbjörn might rather have shared the sentiments of Petrarch when he visited Avignon. Springfield was to Esbjörn a Babylonian Captivity.

Hay later changed his mind about Springfield. He had been a shining light of the Philomathean Society and his brother, Augustus Leonard, wrote later to him as follows: "I wonder if Lincoln ever studied by a 'tallow dip' as you and I did at Springfield when Phelps and Lee argufied on metaphysics, . . . while Herodotus, in original Greek, lay waiting and neglected in the corner to reassert himself, and floor us the next morning before the faculty of I. S. U."

Esbjörn had no such nostalgia for Springfield. He had left it hurriedly in the spring of 1860. He gave the Scandinavians no other choice than to secede from the Synod of Northern Illinois and to organize their own independent synod and establish an institution of higher learning of their own, namely, Augustana College and Theological Seminary.

The withdrawal of the Scandinavians from the Illinois State University dealt it a crippling blow. Again an effort was made to rally the citizens of Springfield to the support of the university. On June 28, 1860, Abraham Lincoln was elected as a trustee to fill the unexpired term of Rev. R. Dodge, a notice of which was carried in the *Illinois State Journal* of July 3, 1860. He was undoubtedly elected because of his national prominence. Because he had many close friends on the Board of Trustees,

8

it is surprising that he had not been chosen a trustee of the university earlier.

Lincoln could not devote any time to the universtiy, his time being taken by the campaign. The Civil War ruined any chances for it to survive the crisis created by schism of the Scandinavians. In 1862 the university had only 70 students, many having taken "French leave" to join the army.

The loyalty of the Swedish immigrants to the name of Lincoln is not to be traced to Springfield. In general it seems that the time of arrival of immigrants to America and their distribution determined their political party loyalties. Those who arrived from 1828 to 1845 formed ties of loyalty to the Democratic party. In 1828, 30,000 immigrants arrived and after 1832 the number fell below 30,000 on only two occasions. Immigration culminated in a tidal wave after 1845 which was checked by the outbreak of the Crimean War and the Panic of 1857. Relatively few of the immigrants prior to 1850 were Swedish, but these like the others tended to favor the Democratic party, if they took an interest in politics.

The Democratic party was the party in power. It was associated with internal improvement projects which provided immigrants with opportunities for employment. It was responsible for liberalizing the federal land policies through which it became possible for immigrants to become farmers. The immigrants were encouraged to take an active part in politics through liberal suffrage laws. The Whig party, on the other hand, remained aloof from the immigrants except for the election of 1840, and with its increased political misfortunes it became plagued by nativism. The few Swedes who had become affiliated with the Democratic party had little influence upon immigrants who arrived after 1850 when a series of political events led to the doom of the old Whig party and the birth of the Republican party. Old loyalties were challenged and new ones were formed as was demonstrated in the political careers of Lincoln and Lyman Trumbull, one a former Whig and the other a Democrat, who forgot old rivalries and jealousies to join the Republican party. It was a party which from its inception appealed to the Scandinavians, and to the Swedes in particular. Most of them had no previous political prejudices.

9

Many of them had settled where New England influences were strong. This was true of Galesburg, Illinois, which had been a hot bed of abolitionist sentiment.

Hemlandet, Det Gamla och Det Nya was conceived in Galesburg a year after the Republican party had entered state politics and a year before it became a national party. Many people had been left adrift politically after the passage of the Kansas-Nebraska Act of 1854. Some who felt particularly insecure and did not wish to see America torn apart over the question of slavery sought to unite a divided America against a common foe, the Roman Catholic Church. To many Swedes this was an adversary which must be fought. But as much as abolitionism and anti-Catholicism appealed to the Swedes, they were not political extremists. The Church exerted a conservative influence upon them which carried over into American politics. But it was not the only influence. Few of the immigrants were interested in the many experimental utopian communities of the last century. They were individualists to whom the opportunities offered by a free society loomed large. They probably did not understand the finer points involved in public policy, but they did have a deep appreciation of democracy. The cities, which witnessed bloody street fighting in countries where the leaven of democracy was working, contributed few immigrants. The revolutionists of 1830 and 1848 spoke of liberty as embracing republican institutions with guarantees of freedom of assembly, speech, and press. The immigrants, prior to 1850, were the sons of the soil who looked upon freedom as a way of life associated with the right to "buy, sell, and bargain, to work or loaf, to become rich or poor." One Swede quoted by Marcus Lee Hansen in *The Immigrant in American History* wrote: "What I like about the country is that the farmer can dismiss his hired hand any day he wants to, and the hired hand can leave when the impulse strikes him. As a result, each is more careful with the respect to the other than in countries where the terms and conditions of service are drawn up in a legal contract."

Freedom was to the immigrant a source of energy and social well being. Few arrived with fantastic illusions of wealth to be won in America. Most wished to preserve what they had. European conditions influenced by the industrial, commercial, and agricultural revolutions did not destroy old class distinctions. A few found in a greater shift from an economy of status to one of money, opportunities for social advancement, but more were threatened by decline in the gradations of society. This might well have been a major factor in emigration from Europe.

The previous political inexperience of the immigrants was a factor which might have led to the Republican fold. They had not enjoyed any political rights of suffrage in Sweden. The Norwegians had arrived earlier and had come from a more "democratic" country than had the Swedes. They soon began to take an active part in American politics. Prior to the publication of *Hemlandet,* in 1855, there had been only two brief unsuccessful efforts to publish a "Scandinavian" newspaper in America. *Hemlandet* was to have rivals, but they too favored the Republican party. They were, however, neither numerous nor important until some years after the Civil War. Dean Theodore C. Blegen, of the University of Minnesota, however, states that the Norwegian-American press had seen the birth of several newspapers and periodicals over a decade and a half before the 1860 election. These newspapers had voiced many diverse political views. Although their existence was stormy and short, they did play an important role in educating the immigrants in the American way of life, and this became the essential function of *Hemlandet.* While more Norwegians than Swedes had become Democrats, their press reflects the significant political realliances in the Northwest associated with a series of events which led to the birth of the Republican party. The Swedes were baptized into the political life of America by the fiery forces which gave rise to that party. The pioneer immigrants viewed life in terms of eternal values. Life was white or black; things were either true or false. Nothing was neutral. Party platforms were measured by the yardstick of the Scripture.

When *Hemlandet* was born in 1855 the Whig party was dead. The Kansas-Nebraska Act was a momentous measure. Opposition to it was spontaneous, and the Republican party came into existence pledged to oppose the extension of slavery. Sectional interests became more marked. The developments appeared to the editor of *Hemlandet* to have turned the once liberal Democratic party into a pro-slavery party. It was no longer waging a battle against a Whig aristocracy and its conservative doctrines.

11

"Who could under these circumstances support the Democratic party?" But in its first national contest the Republican party failed to prevent the election of James Buchanan, although it showed strength. Much of this stemmed from the support of immigrants, and in the next four years Republicans curried their favor.

Many Germans might have found it difficult to accept the Maine Law as an infringement upon their personal liberties, but this was not true of the Swedes touched by the religious awakening. To the founders of the Swedish Lutheran churches in America liberty to act and think was circumscribed. No one was allowed to follow the flesh. There was to be modesty of dress if the conscience were awake. The puritanical influences which were strong in the Republican party appealed to the Swedes. They favored not only laws forbidding the manufacture and sale of liquor but laws calling for a strict observance of the Sabbath. Some Germans feared that the Republican party consisted of members who were nativists. This question was of little significance to the Swedes.

America was a country of great resources that was expanding rapidly. Who was to gain by the westward expansion, Christ or the Devil? Thus, the American people were face to face with basic ideals, a belief in God, a moral law, freedom, and destiny. On almost every point Hasselquist would have disagreed with Henry Thoreau, the author of *Civil Disobedience,* except one, namely, that man must be guided by his conscience. Hasselquist praised the fight of the Know-Nothings against German free thinkers and liberals who had fled from Europe in 1848. But he condemned any form of secrecy. It was an infringement upon the freedom to think and act. Swedish immigrants were poor; poverty had been a factor in their emigration from Sweden. Poverty had taught them the important lesson of thrift. Both husband and wife worked in order to save money which was set aside for the purchase of a home or a farm. *Hemlandet* urged the immigrants to preserve this thrift, add to it American cleanliness, and "work for the Kingdom of God."

In working for the Kingdom of God they could not sanction slavery. It was "ungodly in its foundation." It could not endure in a Christian country and be defended by a sound conscience. But Hasselquist had no answer as to how slavery might be abolished or how the owners might be compensated for loss of property or what would happen to the free Negroes. For this he was taken to task by a Texas Swede, who did share Hasselquist's view that slavery was sinful. *Hemlandet* only replied with what became the usual answers of those who had read *Uncle Tom's Cabin.* Slaves were whipped, burned to death if they struck their masters, deprived of their children, compelled to suffer humiliating sexual relations, and eat unsatisfactory food. All issues were related to the slavery question. This was true of railroad building and all internal improvement projects, and industrial expansion, as well as the progress of free states, and the public land question, which was of special interest to land-hungry, thrifty, hardworking immigrants, who wished to become economically independent.

The editor of *Hemlandet* was an active Republican. A meeting was held in the First Presbyterian Church in Galesburg to nominate delegates for the State Republican Convention to be held in Bloomington, Illinois. Honorable C. W. Brown presided at this meeting while Hasselquist shared the platform with Rev. Edward Beecher and other dignitaries. At the Bloomington Convention, Lincoln showed himself to be the friend of immigrants.

Hasselquist had been in America four years. Some manifestations of American political excitement still offended him. How disturbed he might have been by noisy crowds, parades, flags, slogans, and torches is hard to judge. In a Galesburg parade a banner displaying a cow with the head of Buchanan, and later the burning of an effigy of President Franklin Pierce offended him. He left the crowd to be told later that Buchanan too had been burned.

Two years later committees for Kansas were organized widely in counties and cities as efforts were made to fight the adoption of the Lecompton Constitution. At the Republican Convention in Springfield, Senator Trumbull was praised, Lincoln was chosen to oppose Douglas, and Democrats were criticized for their extravagance. Gustave Koerner presided at the Convention and showed the Germans that the Republican party was not Know-Nothing.

The year of 1858 was an important one in focusing the nation's attention upon Lincoln and in sharpening political issues. *Hemlandet* became more Republican, if possible, without becoming less anti-Democrat. Lincoln carried off victories in the debates at Ottawa and Quincy, August 24, and October 26, 1858. Popular sovereignty was condemned. Slavery was an evil, a question upon which people could not be permitted to express themselves. The day of greatest importance was, as might be expected, the Galesburg debate on October 7, 1858. It occurred on a Thursday and had been anticipated for days by extensive preparations. The rising sun on Thursday was greeted by the firing of a cannon. It was a clear, windy, and cold day. The Swedes gathered outside Hasselquist's church. They had prepared a banner reading LINCOLN—THE SCANDI-NAVIANS FOR FREE LABOR. They organized into two companies with bands and Swedish and American flags. Douglas arrived at 11:00 a.m. Half an hour later Lincoln was greeted by a cheering crowd and the firing of a cannon. Masses of parading humanity appeared from every direction. One group headed by a "Scandinavian band" for Douglas consisted actually of Germans.

Hemlandet was then the only Swedish-American newspaper in Illinois. *Den Svenska Republickanen* published in Galva had a short career. It had found the clerical influences of *Hemlandet* objectionable but had joined hands in promoting the Republican cause of 1856. It did not witness the Lincoln-Douglas debates. Its editor, however, had been a delegate to the Republican State Convention in Springfield which nominated Lincoln as Republican candidate for United States Senate. Its last issue dated July 1, 1858, carried the platform of the Republican party.

Rev. Eric Norelius had started a newspaper for the Minnesota Swedes in 1858. Norelius, a fellow clergyman of Hasselquist, was a member of the Synod of Northern Illinois who chafed at its doctrinal and spiritual laxity. He had feared that if a Republican newspaper were not begun in Minnesota a Democratic one would be started. Norelius was hardly less interested in the Lincoln-Douglas debates than was Hasselquist. He urged the Swedes to form Republican clubs and condemned the Dred Scott decision as being contrary to the Declaration of Independence.

The feelings between Hasselquist and Esbjörn had long been strained. Hasselquist had opposed Esbjörn's appointment to the Scandinavian professorship. Norelius was a young admirer of Esbjörn, and Hasselquist viewed Norelius' venture into journalism with suspicion. To check a possible schism among the little remnant, Hasselquist offered the editorship of *Hemlandet* to Norelius, after which it was moved to Chicago at the beginning of 1859. After a year Norelius surrendered the editorship to Rev. Erland Carlsson.

Frihetsvännen (Friend of liberty) appeared in January, 1859. It declared itself to be non-sectarian, but before long it became evident that it was an organ of the Swedish Baptists. At first the paper exhibited great tact but soon the two rival Swedish newspapers engaged in common name-calling. *Frihetsvännen* had no intention of becoming a blind partisan Republican spokesman as had *Hemlandet*, which "cloaked its partisanship with priestly treachery and deceit." But how could *Frihetsvännen* remain non-partisan in a struggle over moral issues? The political situation forced *Frihetsvännen* to take a firm stand as a Republican newspaper. It, too, began to disseminate bitter propaganda against the Democrats spiced with as deep religious prejudices as those of *Hemlandet.*

The strength exhibited by the Republicans in 1858 gave cause for confidence. The party was older, its platform well defined, while the Democrats were split into pro- and anti-Douglas factions. An important lesson had been learned from 1858, namely, that the Republicans must gain control of the state legislatures. The movement to organize Republican clubs was stimulated by a Chicago city election.

Real political excitement began with the Illinois State Republican Convention, which met at Decatur on May 9, 1860. Here there was much enthusiasm for Lincoln. A banner was brought onto the floor of the convention between two rails which, it was said, had been split by "Old Abe" in 1830, when he worked ten miles south of Decatur. Lincoln was in good humor. Referring to the large rails, he said that he had split them or others as large. The Illinois delegates were instructed to vote for Lincoln at the coming National Convention in Chicago.

The Republican platform received much attention in the pages of *Hemlandet,* and the party's position in regard to naturalization was featured. *Hemlandet* might have preferred to see William Henry Seward nominated at the convention. It was felt that Seward had earned the nomination. Yet, Lincoln was a strong candidate. His principles had been

15

clearly defined when he clashed with Douglas in 1858. Perhaps, it is worthy of observation that *Hemlandet* stressed Lincoln's success as a lawyer and not his humble origin. Swedish social prejudices might have asserted themselves in this case. Thus, it was far more important that Lincoln was called "Honest Abe" than the "railsplitter." But *Hemlandet* would have accepted any candidate of the Republican party in 1860.

Because German immigrants were more numerous than the Scandinavians, the Republican party—in angling for the foreign vote—favored German delegates to state Republican conventions in Iowa, Illinois, Minnesota, and Wisconsin. Carl Schurz, who felt that he represented at the National Republican Convention 300,000 German votes, was placed in charge of the "foreign department of the Naitonal Committee." Its function was to win the immigrant vote. He condemned measures hostile to these and advocated a liberal homestead act as well as firm opposition to the extension of slavery. He suggested the enrollment of prominent citizens—who were German, Scandinavian, and Dutch—to speak to the immigrants in their native tongues. One major task of these speakers was to stress that the Republican party had always been friendly to the immigrants. Schurz and his cohorts pointed out that the amendment sponsored by Republicans to the Constitution of Massachusetts was directed against the Irish and the Catholics.

The country had by no means recovered from the Panic of 1857. The economic hardships had inflamed mistrust among the Lutherans of the Synod of Northern Illinois, strained the small and inadequate resources of the Illinois State University, hurried the establishment of a new Scandinavian church, given rise to Augustana College, drained the resources of *Frihetsvännen,* endangered *Hemlandet* by bankruptcy, threatened immigrants with the loss of their homes and farms, and stimulated religious prejudices and racial bigotry. Douglas was said to have been a Catholic, and if this were not true, he probably married one and could count upon the support of ninety-nine per cent of all Catholics in America. The Republican party, a hodge podge of Free Soilers, Whigs, Know-Nothings, Abolitionists, "Puritan" temperance advocates with the strong support of Protestants of the North and an army of immigrants, revived the old Whig stand on the protective tariff and went to considerable pains in educating the immigrant in the ideals of Henry Carey. According to *Hemlandet* the Democratic party was corrupt, split, and impotent and a growing feeling of insecurity in America expressed itself in "tyranny, sensationalism, moral decline, ignorance, spread of crime, and fears of safety of life and property." When the Fourth of July was celebrated *Hemlandet* took the opportunity to expound the gospel of the Republican faith. And it became a holy gospel! It was built upon Protestant foundations. When a Democrat became a Republican he was "converted" and "saved." Why should not the Swedes who loved liberty and freedom rejoice at the thought of salvation for all mankind? The duties of the Swedes to the "enslaved" Negroes were self-evident. But to prevent a great shock upon society, the gradual but complete abolition of slavery was necessary. This could be accomplished calmly by practical measures after a Republican victory. The religious fervor among the Swedes is illustrated by their campaign hymn of 1860. It contained twelve stanzas, three of which have been translated as follows:

> Ye noble sons of the North,
> To the campaign now we go.
> The banner that we carry,
> its legend reads thus:
> "For freedom, right, and truth"
> We will raise our voice.

> "For freedom, right, and truth,
> and Swedish yeoman faith"
> Did our brave Gustavus Adolph
> Risk his life and blood.
> We who are his sons
> Will go the way he trod,
> Though it should be our fate
> To receive the same sad end.

> And now that at our head
> Lincoln leads the advance,
> Should we then stand back?
> Nay, forward in closed ranks,
> And let us vote as one man
> For noble Abraham Lincoln
> To be our President.

17

It is difficult to say what influence Carl Schurz might have had upon the Swedes. He was an effective speaker. Yet, by no means did all of the Germans support the Republican party. The *New Ulm Pioneer* stated that 73 German newspapers were Republican, 35 supported Douglas, 15 Breckinridge, 10 Bell, while 10 expressed no definite political stand. *Hemlandet* filled its columns for several issues with Schurz' address given at St. Louis on August 1, 1860, and it urged its readers to obtain copies of the speech in order that it might be circulated among the few who might still be Democrats.

Schurz might have influenced the strategy of the Republicans in organizing the immigrants into local clubs for their participation in mass meetings and rallies. *Hemlandet* and *Frihetsvännen* urged the immigrants to either join or form Republican clubs. Where the Swedes were less numerous they joined the "Wide-Awake" organizations. In either instance political activity made the immigrants feel that they were Americans. They belonged. They wished to be both liked and respected and these desires reflected themselves in their enthusiastic participation in the campaign of 1860. They listened to orations in both Swedish and English, joined in noisy parades, carried flags and banners, cheered for Lincoln and the Republican cause. The Swedish churches were often focal points outside of which the Swedes would gather in preparing themselves for the parades.

Rallies and parades were numerous. *Hemlandet* estimated that from 10,000 to 20,000 persons attended a Republican rally at Galesburg. Swedes arrived in Galesburg from Knoxville and Wautauga. They gathered outside the First Lutheran Church. The spire of the church was decorated with many flags. The major speaker to address the Swedes was Charles J. Sundell who described Douglas as a fox and Lincoln as honesty itself. Sundell and C. J. Stolbrand were perhaps the most popular of the Swedish-speaking campaign orators. Most of the clergymen of the Swedish Lutheran churches served as campaign orators, appearing on the same platforms as Sundell and Stolbrand.

The Swedes also listened to many Americans including Cassius M. Clay, Owen Lovejoy, William Kellogg, Joseph Knox, Robert G. Ingersoll, and others. At various rallies they tried to secure special attention

ABRAHAM LINCOLN
In 1860

L. P. ESBJÖRN
A founder of Augustana College
President, 1860-1863

T. N. HASSELQUIST
A founder of Augustana College
President, 1863-1891

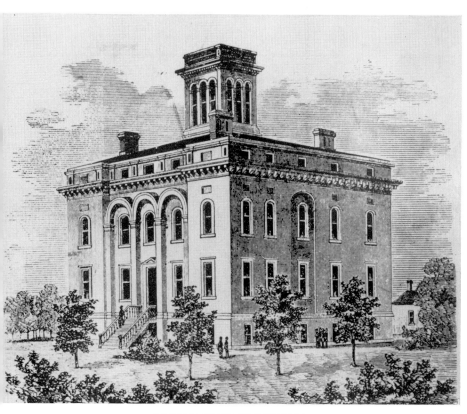

ILLINOIS STATE UNIVERSITY
Springfield, 1860

A RAILROAD TRAIN OF THE 1850'S

LYMAN TRUMBULL
U. S. Senator from Illinois
1855-1873

THE REPUBLICANS IN NOMINATING CONVENTION IN THEIR WIGWAM AT CHICAGO, MAY, 1860.

WILLIAM H. SEWARD
U. S. Secretary of State
1861-1869

JAMES G. RANDALL, 1881-1953
A friend, teacher, and Lincoln scholar

through number, enthusiasm, cleverly decorated wagons, young women dressed to appear as representatives of the various states, large bands, conspicuous banners on which such slogans as EQUALITY REGARDLESS OF ORIGIN OF BIRTH might be inscribed. At Galesburg they boasted that they were the largest group represented, and that many at the great rally who were Democrats became "converted."

At Bishop Hill there was another of the many rallies in which Swedes had an opportunity of displaying their strength as they came from Andover, Walnut Grove, Victoria, Galesburg, and Princeton. This rally attracted 8,000 persons. On October 5, 1860, Senator Seward spoke in Chicago and the Swedes were urged to attend. Excursions on railroads were organized. A special invitation was sent out to various Swedish Republican clubs to attend the Chicago rally by the Swedish Republican Club of Chicago. *Hemlandet* estimated that from 75,000 to 100,000 visitors were brought to Chicago by the great Republican mass meeting. Perhaps 10,000 Wide-Awakes added color to the city by their uniforms. It looked almost as if every one was a "Wide-Awake"; certainly, many Swedes were. But men, women, and children had taken advantage of the excursions to get to Chicago and to participate in or watch the parade. There were also 500 "Lincoln Rangers" on horseback in a parade with customary bands, banners, flags, and torches. The Swedish Republican Club of Chicago was represented by seventy-two members. They carried both Swedish and American flags and a banner with the inscription on one side: LIBERTY AND RIGHT FOREVER: EXPANSION OF SLAVERY NEVER. On the other side it read: SWEDISH REPUBLICANS OF CHICAGO. This group marched past the office of *Hemlandet* where three cheers were given. At Republican mass meetings all over northern Illinois, where Swedes were to be found, they brought "honor" upon their people. In Princeton, Ill., on October 4, 1860, the mass meeting, as elsewhere, was a huge success. Perhaps 8,000 or 10,000 people attended, but in the procession some 250 Swedes received special attention. They were directed by a man named A. A. Skenlund. On one wagon the Swedes had thirty-three young women dressed in white, wearing green and white wreaths on their heads and ribbon girdles with the names of the different states and one woman with the name of Kansas, not yet admitted as a state.

Each woman carried a Lincoln-Hamlin flag. The Swedish procession was headed by the American flag followed by the Swedish one.

The flavor of revival camp was present at Republican mass meetings. Prayers were said, hymns were sung, the Bible was quoted, and the campaign orator was no less zealous in calling upon God than had been the old circuit rider. The election of 1860 was a Pentecostal experience to the Swedish immigrants. The gospel of the Republican party was expounded from the pulpits, as if it were a part of the creeds.

The religious symbolism of the Swedes was often in evidence as was the case at a Princeton rally. The Swedes carried a banner in the parade showing on one side the capitol of the United States being entered by a courageous lion having the head of Abraham Lincoln, and a wolf with the head of Douglas and a tail inscribed with popular sovereignty, and a tiger with the head of Breckinridge turning away in flight. On the other side of the banner the wolf and the tiger fired upon the capitol with a cannon, but the lion with one fell swoop of his tail destroyed the cannon and threw the wolf and the tiger to the ground.

There is no need to picture the joy of Swedes over Lincoln's victory. The Swedes had done their duty. Few, if any, were Democrats. Seemingly desperate the Democrats had on the eve of the election published a campaign fly sheet in Swedish, which *Hemlandet* was quick to point out had been published in a German print shop! It was poorly written and contained many humorous typographical errors. "Landlösa" meaning "landless" appeared as "tandlösa" meaning "toothless."

How is the Republican propaganda in pages of *Hemlandet* to be weighed? Was it not true that every day in 1860 was much like every other day, that people married, built homes, begot children, tilled the soil, worked in shops, worried, prayed, and worshipped in a world which centered on the self while the big world on the outside could not be comprehended? The pages of *Hemlandet* abound in news from the world of the immigrants in which politics played no role. The little remnant had launched a church body of its own in 1860 which could be sustained only if men were trained and educated to serve the spiritual needs of the immigrants. Attention was, therefore, focused upon the struggling educational institution temporarily housed in a Norwegian Lutheran Church in

Chicago, where Esbjörn continued to serve as a teacher. Contributions to the Seminary were mentioned in *Hemlandet*. Farmers near Chicago brought eggs, butter, meat, pork, and potatoes to the College and Seminary. Others sent a dollar or two to Esbjörn; a widow her mite; a spinster endowed with more worldly goods sent seventy-five cents. O. C. T. Andreen was sent to Sweden on a holy mission to enlist support for the College and Seminary. He left America in the midst of the political campaign. The little remnant followed him to the railroad station in Chicago and wished him the blessings of God.

Hemlandet gave no sign of fears that the Union itself had been threatened by Lincoln's victory until in December of 1860, and in January of 1861 it doubted that it was possible to avert a civil war. It seemed perhaps to be the only way in which slavery could be abolished. War was better than a compromise with evil. Republicans who favored a modified Crittenden amendment were regarded as traitors. Indeed, the conflict seemed irrepressible. When Lincoln called for 75,000 volunteers, *Hemlandet,* once again the only Swedish-American newspaper, regretted that he had not called for them earlier. The oncoming Civil War seemed to *Hemlandet* to be "God's plan to blot out slavery." The Swedes were urged to volunteer for the cause of union and liberty. L. P. Esbjörn took the occasion to preach a sermon on "Liberty, justice, and truth." Hasselquist urged progress for the cause of the Union. Swedish volunteers inspired by patriotism changed their names from Swensson, and Pettersson to McCase, Peters, Hawkins, and the like.

The immigrants had been prodigious. Every year more of them had arrived and our foreign born population had grown. They were young and sturdy. They provided the brawn necessary for a more rapid westward expansion; they built canals and roads, tilled the soil and manned new factories and shops. They built churches and schools. But no immigrant college nor any other college could provide the ingredients necessary to fulfill the dream of Thomas Jefferson of an American with "the body of an athlete and the mind of an Aristotle." The westward expansion added to the American dilemma. New communications did not bring the North and the South any closer; plows guided by strong hands of sons of the European soil dug deeper furrows; new factories and shops

21

forged a hotter iron for the plow; loud voices in many tongues sang hymns of liberty, and new institutions of learning accentuated cultural and ideological cleavages. Among the immigrants there were intellectuals, graduates of old and venerated universities, but an anti-intellectual climate called for only one solution of the American dilemma, and this was by the sword. Brother turned against brother, and of no record was the immigrant more proud than that of his service in the uniform of the Blue.

With Walt Whitman, the immigrants could pronounce the Civil War good. Men had died for their ideals. The Battle-Hymn of the Republic became their hymn.

"Mine eyes have seen the glory of the coming of the Lord:
He is trampling out the vintage where the grapes of wrath are stored;
He hath loosed the fateful lightning of his terrible swift sword;
His truth is marching on."

Had the Almighty had His own purposes?

T. HARRY WILLIAMS

Lincoln and

The Causes of the Civil War

Without the institution of slavery, and the colored race as a basis, the war could not have an existence. (Lincoln in an "Address on Colonization to a Deputation of Negroes," Aug. 14, 1862)

The historians of the Civil War have done an admirable if sometimes too complete a job of surveying the conflict that is the pivotal event in our history. They have depicted in detail most of the main men and movements and some of the minor ones as well. Taken as a whole, their work is marked by insight and intelligence and a deft sureness of touch. That is, they have known what they were looking for, where to find it, and how to present it. But this certainty disappears when they come to deal with the causes of the war. It has to be reported that historians have not been notably successful in describing the factors that brought on the struggle or the motives moving such central actors in the drama as Abraham Lincoln. This failure is not surprising. The methodology of history—which elevates reliance on documents above all else—does not lend itself to interpretation of the elusive emotions that lead men to fight for a cause. And unfortunately for historians, men who have fought rarely leave behind them neat records of why they drew the sword. It has been suggested that historians can enlarge their understanding of the nature of war by utilizing the materials and methods of related disciplines in the social sciences. This is probably correct, but the results of efforts in this direction by some historians have not been too promising. The craft has not as yet mastered the technique of exploiting the related disciplines. Possibly the historian who wishes to learn more about war should begin by learning more about human nature, about man inside himself and outside himself, in the present and in the past.

23

The literature on the war's causation may have its shortcomings, but it is formidable in size. If we had to choose a word to characterize this body of writing, it would be controversy. Probably no other episode in our history has evoked so much hot difference of opinion in the cool community of scholarship. The reasons for these freewheeling brawls are obvious. When historians discuss the causes of the Civil War, they are dealing with fundamental forces in our national life, with issues that continue to affect society to this day—sectional divisions, majority and minority rights, and the thorny problem of race. These are things that matter to most people, and they have mattered to historians. Inevitably historians are influenced by the culture of their time; in interpreting the past they will necessarily employ value standards of the present. The headlong rush of history in the last three decades, altering accepted criteria almost overnight, has promoted confusion and controversy in the historical world. Speaking perhaps too generally, in the 1930's and early 1940's historical writing about the Civil War and its background tended to be, in varying degree, of course, with different writers, pro-southern, pro-agrarian, pro-Democratic. Now in our day, a troubled time when people seek for positive values in the American past, the same writing tends to be pro-northern, pro-industrial, pro-Republican. The pendulum may be about to swing too far.

Scholarly controversy can be highly beneficial to all concerned and to the cause of history itself. It stimulates self-examination, provokes thinking along original lines, and may result in the presentation of new viewpoints. Moreover, all historians are better for having been subjected to criticism. Even so great a historian as the late Douglas Southall Freeman would have been greater if his books had been exposed to some intelligent analysis by reviewers. But differences among Civil War historians are likely to go beyond the confines of abstract argument and become bitterly personal. Thus one writer speaks of the "fulmination of Owsley, Coulter, and their ilk." Another, aiming at Avery Craven, a frequent target in this verbal warfare, charges that Craven has used his talents "to enchant readers, under the guise of historical and scientific objectivity, in an obsolescent and tyrannical cause," namely slavery. It is evident that we have here something more than just a divergence over the meaning of history. I happen to disagree with some of the views about the war. held by the late J. G. Randall, but this would not lead me to impugn the basis of Professor Randall's scholarship. The depth and the frequent rancor of the current controversy suggest that it springs from fundamental forces in the American past and in present American culture.

In 1954 Thomas J. Pressly summarized the various schools of historical thought on the causes of the sectional conflict in a book, *Americans Interpret Their Civil War*. Although all of Professor Pressly's judgments are not to be accepted, his system of classification offers a convenient point of departure. Certainly his book demonstrates how the culture of particular periods influences historical writing. Disregarding the partisan writers of both sides who appeared right after the war, we find the first genuine historical school emerging in the 1890's. This group, represented by such men as James Ford Rhodes, Edward Channing, and Woodrow Wilson, Pressly denotes as the Nationalists. Unlike the early partisans and also unlike some later writers, the Nationalists did not impute war guilt to either section. The Civil War came because of fundamental causes, notably slavery, they said, implying, at least, that it was irrepressible. But neither side was to blame; each fought for what it thought was right. The nationalist interpretation was almost universally accepted until the era of World War I. Its popularity was obviously rooted in prevailing conditions of American culture. This was a time of expanding nationalism, when the United States was advancing to the status of a world power. The South could take pride that it was a part of a mighty nation, a nation that had been saved by the Civil War. Nor was the nation divided by tensions on the racial issue. The majority North had abandoned its effort to determine the status of the Negro, and the minority South could feel that it had salvaged something from the war.

But in the 1920's a new school arose to challenge and eventually displace the Nationalists. The founder and inspiring force of this group was Charles A. Beard, expounder of the influence of economic determinism on the course of history, and we may accurately term it the Beardian school. Beard agreed with the Nationalists that the Civil War was the irrepressible result of fundamental causes. But the causes had nothing to do with slavery or concepts of government, he insisted. Two rival economic societies, one industrial and the other agricultural, had met in a confrontation that could end only in total triumph for one. The victory of the North was to Beard the "Second American Revolution." Although the cultural influences behind Beardian thought are not as clear as is the case with the Nationalists, it is evident that both the master and his followers were affected by the main currents of their time: the tensions and dislocations attending the rise of big business and the increasing emphasis on the importance of economics engendered by the progressive movement. Possibly the Beardian historians suffered the same frustrations that plagued progressive politicians who did not quite understand all the implications of the shiny economic order burgeoning around them.

The Beardian interpretation won sudden and wide acceptance and was popular for years; indeed, it still has adherents. But it never became a common concept, as had the Nationalist analysis, because almost immediately it encountered the competition of still other schools. In the 1930's certain southern historians, notably the late Frank L. Owsley and the late Charles Ramsdell, advanced their thesis about the cause of the war. These men, called by Pressly the "Southern Vindicators," reiterated that the conflict had been irrepressible—but for reasons entirely different from those suggested by the Nationalists and the Beardians. The war was the outcome of the aggressive actions of the majority section, the North. The attempt of the North to dominate the nation was, in Professor Owsley's words, a manifestation of "egocentric sectionalism." It is significant that this view was put forward at a time when new pressures were beating on the South: the push of industry into the section, altering the old mores of a rural people, and the revival of tensions on the racial issue. Significant, too, is that in the writings of the Vindicators we find the first questioning of the values of nationalism, the first doubts about the unifying results of the Civil War.

These same doubts—was the American nation worth a war?—were expressed more strongly in the writings of another school that appeared concurrently with the Vindicators and that gained a much wider acceptance. The historians in this group are commonly known as the Revisionists, although they did not hold completely common views. We can best get at revisionism by examining the ideas of the school's most representa-

26

tive figure, J. G. Randall. According to Randall, the war was not irrepressible or the result of fundamental causes. It had not been caused by slavery or economic grievances or state rights or diverse civilizations. Searching for a word to account for it, Randall suggested "fanaticism, misunderstanding, misrepresentation, or perhaps politics." It was a needless war, brought on by inept or perhaps evil men, by, in a phrase made famous by Randall, "a blundering generation." This conviction of Randall's invested that part of his biography of Lincoln dealing with the 1850's with a curious quality. He could not sympathize with Lincoln's position in the sectional controversy, and perhaps without Randall realizing it Douglas became the hero of the story. Randall's treatment of the Civil War reflected a general outlook on war common to liberal intellectuals of the time. Wars were hardly ever caused by fundamental factors, Randall stated, because war was an aberration in human conduct. Implicit in Randall's whole argument was the idea that anything was preferable to war. Therefore both sides and particularly the majority North should have made a compromise that would have prevented the Civil War. The revisionist analysis obviously was related to the liberal disillusionment with war as an instrument of national policy and with nationalism as a breeder of war.

The revisionist thesis had a tremendous impact on historical thinking about the Civil War. Indeed, it was more widely accepted than any explanation of the war except that of the Nationalists. Not until after World War II was it seriously challenged. That conflict changed the whole liberal intellectual concept of war. Now it appeared that tensions were not as easily resolved as once thought possible, that war was an inescapable outlet from some situations, and that war was preferable to some compromises. Moreover, the emergence first of the Nazi menace and in the postwar world of the Communist menace moved men to ascribe new values to nationalism (a strong and united America) and to industrialism (the productive American economy). One result of the new persuasion was to turn historians to take another look at the war that had preserved the American nation. Most of them concluded that its outcome had been fortunate. Some of them looked at its causes and decided that the Revisionists were wrong. The first attacks on revisionism came from

Bernard DeVoto and A. M. Schlesinger, Jr. They charged that it was not enough to dismiss the causes of the war as inconsequential or to say that people had become needlessly excited over artificial issues. The job of the historian was to explain why the issues were considered important, why people had become excited. As the critics increased in number, they began to develop a thesis of their own as to the war's causation. Pressly calls these writers the New Nationalists, and for an obvious reason. Their analysis resembled closely that of the first school. They said that the war had fundamental causes and that the biggest of these was slavery, although they put more emphasis on slavery as part of a continuing race problem than the first Nationalists. While admitting that the war was a tragedy, they could see no alternative unless the South had been willing to abandon its peculiar institution. They were impatient with Southerners for not yielding to the antislavery impulse, seeming to think that a people can surmount their culture. It was no accident that the new school arose not only in a period of resurgent nationalism but at a time when racial pressures and tensions were greater than at any time since Reconstruction.

Whatever historians have thought about the sectional controversy, it was a reality, and it was very real to those engaged in it. We have only to look at almost any statements by leaders on either side to catch the depth of the emotions of the period. To Jefferson Davis there was nothing artificial in the situation: "If this were the result of passion, . . . I should have hopes which I cannot now cherish. If it were the mere outbreak of violence, I should see some prospect for its subsidence. But, considering it as I do, the cold, calculating purpose of those who seek for sectional domination, I see nothing short of conquest on the one side, or submission on the other. . . . It is no longer the clamor of a noisy fanaticism, but the steady advance of a self-sustaining power to the goal of unlimited supremacy." The issues were just as plain to William H. Seward: "Shall I tell you what this collision means? They who think that it is accidental, unnecessary, the work of interested or fanatical agitators, and therefore ephemeral, mistake the case altogether. It is an irrepressible conflict between opposing and enduring forces. . . ." Historians who have written about the war's background have been too prone to judge by their own standards the importance of issues in the 1850's, to dismiss as mere abstractions the problems that excited the people of those years. And yet abstractions are the things people have always fought for. Said a Charlottesville, Virginia, editor on the eve of 1861: "There is a habit of speaking derisively of going to war for *an idea*—an abstraction—something which you cannot see. . . . An idea is exactly the thing that we would fight for. . . . For this idea of State honor . . . we would convulse this Union from centre to circumference." Antebellum leaders commonly cast the issues of the day in abstract form, and these men—Davis, Seward, Lincoln—were not exactly fools.

If, then, the controversy between the sections was real and meaningful, what were some of the divisive issues? Those historians who stress economic variances obviously have something of a case. The economic systems of the North and the South differed markedly, and the two sections had clashing economic aspirations. It was an economic issue, the tariff, that stirred South Carolina to the extreme of nullification in 1832. In the 1840's and 1850's the South reacted strongly against the Whig and Republican program of having the national government stimulate the economy with subsidies and special legislation. And northern economic interests reacted just as strongly against southern opposition to this program. The leaders of both sides were well aware of the stakes involved in the competition for economic primacy. Jefferson Davis frankly told the North: "You desire to weaken the political power of the Southern states; and why? Because you want, by an unjust system of legislation, to promote the industry of the New England states, at the expense of the people of the South and their industry." With equal frankness, John Sherman detailed the meaning of the Republican victory in 1860: "We know very well that the great objects which those who elected Mr. Lincoln expect him to accomplish will be to secure to free labor its just right to the Territories . . . ; to protect . . . by wise revenue laws the labor of our people; to secure the public lands to actual settlers . . . ; to develop the internal resources of the country by opening new means of communication between the Atlantic and the Pacific . . . ".

Also able to present a case are the proponents of the thesis that the

29

war resulted from a conflict of cultures. According to this view, the North and the South represented social systems so dissonant that neither could live with the other. Social differences certainly existed, although there may be something to the surmise that they were important only because of their sparsity. That is, the differences were just enough to be apparent, to convince each side it was possible to convert the other to its standards. The fact that both sides spoke the same language meant that they could understand these variations and boast of their superiority. And boast they did, always loudly and sometimes brutally. Thus the *Atlantic Monthly*, discussing the incongruity of the South's dominating the national government, said: "That the intelligent, educated, and civilized portion of a race should consent to the sway of their ignorant, illiterate, and barbarian companions in the commonwealth, and this by reason of that uncouth barbarism, is an astonishment, and should be a hissing to all beholders everywhere." On the other hand, Southerners were accustomed to vaunting the merits of their aristocratic social system. Cried one orator: "But here there is the perfect possibility. That which, among foreign men, distinguishes the noble and the peer, distinguishes the people in all the states and cities of the South. They are of a ruling race . . . they are braced by the sentiments of that condition—and among men so situated—among men without a master, but with the tone and temper of a master class, it is that we may justly look for centres of correct opinion."

Reading all this gasconade, one wonders if those expressing it really believed everything they said—or did they have some secret doubts or perhaps some hidden envy of the system they attacked? Without a doubt, the South, the key section in the controversy, had a bad minority complex, and with some reason. Since the founding of the republic, the South had slipped proportionally in population and hence in power in those areas of the national government where power was based on numbers, the House of Representatives and the electoral college. In 1790 the South had 49.9 per cent of the total population and 40.1 per cent of the white population; by 1860 the same figures were respectively 39.1 and 29.9 per cent. The South had approximately 45 per cent of the votes in the House of Representatives and the electoral college in 1790, but only 35 per cent in 1860. Even in the Senate, the South had lost a position of equality. In 1850 the number of slave states and free states had been equal, fifteen each. During the next decade three free but no slave states entered the Union. The South was also falling behind in economic progress. Although the region could not complain after 1846 that it was exploited by the tariff, it suffered the inevitable penalty of any producer of raw materials cast in competition with a maker of finished goods. In all the indices that told of national wealth the South was steadily losing ground.

The South was a minority and highly conscious of its status. It was also conscious that it was a minority with a social system which was different—different not only from the system of the nation of which it was a part but different from that of the whole Western world. In analyzing southern psychology, we cannot emphasize too much that slavery and the culture of the slave states were not under just national but also worldwide attack. Put most simply and starkly, the world community disapproved of the South, and expressed its disapproval almost constantly for thirty years before 1860. We cannot measure the effects of this universal censure on the southern mind without getting into the tricky business of mass psychology, but the impact must have been tremendous. We do know that thoughtful Southerners realized the insulation of their section. Said one, H. A. Washington: "For all must admit that the Social System of Virginia is . . . a peculiar system—unlike most of the social systems by which it is surrounded—a sort of anomaly in our times. It has no parallel except in the other slaveholding states . . . , and when closely inspected, looks very much like the remnant of an older civilization—a fragment of the feudal system floating about here on the bosom of the nineteenth century." Another, William Harper, told his people that they could expect no hearing before the tribunal of the civilized world, "insulated as we are by this institution, and cut off . . . from the communion and sympathies of the world by which we are surrounded, . . . and exposed continually to their animadversions . . ." One can surmise that many defenders of slavery really wished that things were otherwise, that the South was more at one with the culture that "surrounded" it.

Historians have given minute attention to the South's feeling of separateness as a cause of the sectional division and of eventual civil war.

31

They have tended to neglect the opposite side of the coin, the force that produced the southern reaction—the spirit or the mood of nationalism. Nationalism was one of the dominating drives of the nineteenth century, as the history of Europe attests. That it was a dynamic influence in American thought can be seen in many sources, particularly in the speeches and state papers of its supreme American exponent, Abraham Lincoln. Nationalism in the United States was an especially puissant force because, as Avery Craven has emphasized, it appeared simultaneously with the industrial revolution. That is, the mood of nationalism coincided with a great transforming economic change that had the effect of interlocking the various parts of society and hence making them interdependent. The revolution in transportation and communication, accomplished by means of the railroad, the steamboat, the telegraph, and the power press, was converting the country into an indivisible whole. In 1800 a trip from New York to St. Louis required over three weeks; by 1850 it could be made in twelve days. In 1850 it took 139 days to cross the continent from New York to San Francisco. By 1877 the required time would be cut to eight days and by 1900 to four. The instrumentalities of technology, almost mechanistic in their impact, precipitated the sections into a sudden and for some an uncomfortable unity. Indeed, many of the defiant expressions of the South in the decade of the fifties were but the reactions of a people who sensed they were being pressed in a direction they did not want to go by perhaps inevitable forces.

We do not know how exactly people of the time realized all the implications of the economic revolution, but, as with so many aspects of the sectional controversy, they were more aware of events than historians have sometimes supposed. Said Stephen A. Douglas: "The application of steam power to transportation and travel has brought the remotest limits of the confederacy, now comprising twenty-six states (if we are permitted to count by time instead of distance) much nearer to the center than when there were but thirteen. The revolution is progressing, and the facilities and rapidity of communication are increasing in a much greater ratio than our territory or population."

We come back to the inevitable question about the controversy between the sections. Was it real, to Lincoln and Davis and other men of the time? Were the issues actual ones or artificial ones? Those historians who have written off the argument as much ado about nothing or as a show got up by the politicians have centered their case around the possibility of slavery entering the territories, the question that most agitated the people of the 1850's. Clearly, say the historians, slavery could not and would not have advanced beyond its existing limits. It would not have been profitable in the territories, indeed, was not very profitable in the South. It had reached the natural limits of its expansion; geography and economics had enacted a law excluding it from the territories. The conclusions drawn from this line of reasoning are interesting. Either the American people had for some unaccountable reason become unreasonably excited about an issue that had no importance—or the whole business was a phoney engineered by politicians like Abraham Lincoln to get the spoils of office. Some historians were kind enough to say that perhaps the politicians were not artful but only inept.

Probably slavery would not have expanded beyond the South because of the operation of natural laws of economics. But the supposition that it would not—or could not—is not quite as apparent as it has seemed. Most studies of the profitability of slavery have been based on the accounting concept. By this standard, the return a planter could have made on his property if he had invested the same capital in another venture was deducted from his yearly profit. Whatever validity the accounting method may have as a measuring system, it lacks realism as a tool for historians. Planters did not use it in calculating their returns, and it had no influence on southern thinking about the economics of slavery. But the accounting concept led historians to believe that slavery was not profitable, in the sense that its rate of return was very low. A recent study by A. H. Conrad and John Meyer (*Journal of Political Economy*, April, 1958), casts doubt on all previous analyses. Employing an economic concept, Conrad and Meyer attempt to measure the profitability of slavery in terms of modern capital theory. They conclude that the rate of return on male slave capital employed in the field averages between five and seven per cent and that the rate on female slave capital, from field work and procreation, ran as high as eight per cent. These figures, say the authors, compare favorably with the returns on investments in other forms of property. If Conrad and Meyer are right, slavery was indeed profitable. Of course, the question of profitability works in two ways. It can be argued that slavery, vital and dynamic, would seek to expand into new areas to reap enlarged returns. Just as logically, it can be argued that it would stay where the returns were certain. But we can be certain of one thing: slavery in the 1850's did not seem a dying institution to Southerners nor was it so regarded by such northern observers as Abraham Lincoln.

The thesis that slavery could not have expanded out of the South derives almost wholly from an article by the late Charles W. Ramsdell (although many historians who stated the thesis may not have realized its source). Ramsdell contended that slavery had reached its natural limit of expansion by the 1850's. There was no place for it to go; hence all the opposition to its expansion was unnecessary, an unreal stand against an unlikely event. But it must be emphasized that Ramsdell placed his argument on only one economic base: slavery had achieved its limits of growth because cotton had reached its limits of extension. That is, slavery would not be profitable where cotton was not profitable. It does not follow, however, that slave labor could be used only in cotton culture. Slavery was exceedingly variable and had many economic possibilities. Slaves could be used, as they were in certain places, in manufacturing and in almost any kind of agricultural operation. It is not beyond possibility that if slavery had not been abolished gangs of slaves might have been organized as migratory workers in the cultivation of wheat on the western plains.

Lincoln and other opponents of slavery believed that slavery possessed the power to expand, and historians have scoffed at their fears. But we should note that supporters of slavery thought it had almost infinite economic possibilities, and said so frequently and openly. George Fitzhugh urged the superiority of slave labor on northern industrialists and predicted that some day slavery would dominate the nation. Jefferson Davis thus described the capacities of slavery: "I hold that the pursuit of gold-washing and mining is better adapted to slave labor than any other . . . I also maintain that [slavery] is particularly adapted to an agriculture which depends upon irrigation." Such statements are extremely important in the story of the sectional controversy. It does not matter that Fitzhugh and

34

Davis may have been wrong. What does matter is that men like Lincoln may have believed they were right.

Today we can see that the odds were against slavery spreading appreciably beyond the South. If for no other reason, the relatively limited number of slaves would have prevented an unlimited expansion. But looking at all the factors in the situation, can we be as sure of some things as we have been? Can we, for example, be certain that slavery could not have existed in Kansas, that natural forces would have made Kansas a free state? Is it not possible that the Buchanan administration might have brought Kansas in as a slave state—if there had not been an organized Republican opposition? We think that slavery could not have existed in Kansas, at least for any significant period of time, but we cannot be absolutely certain. And if we cannot, we should not easily assume that Lincoln and those Republicans who said slavery was about to take over Kansas and other territories either were deceived or were deceivers.

More than any Republican, Lincoln stressed that slavery was on the march, that it was aggressively reaching out into new areas: the territories and possibly the free states themselves. He did not say positively that this thrust was the result of a deliberate plan, of an organized movement, but he hinted strongly at the possibility. We know today that there was no purposeful all-southern effort to extend slavery. Some Southerners, it is true, belligerently demanded *Lebensraum* for slavery, even at the expense of a foreign war to annex regions in Latin America. But most Southerners would have preferred to let the question of actual expansion lie dormant. They might talk firmly and bravely, especially for northern consumption, about the right to take their slave property into the territories, but they were contending for an abstraction. In private or in cooler moments they would have admitted that only a fraction of the territories might conceivably be won for slavery. The South, in some of the crises of the 1850's, notably in the furore surrounding the Kansas-Nebraska Act, was not the aggressor, but permitted itself to be jockeyed into a position of apparent aggression by a few extremist politicians, most of them from the border states.

Lincoln, then, was wrong in thinking that slavery was moving on to

35

new conquests, and especially wrong in suspecting that there was some kind of organized scheme to push it into new areas. But the conclusions that many historians have drawn from this judgment need analysis. These conclusions are, whether or not they were so bluntly stated, that Lincoln and other Republicans were, if not fools, certainly not very perceptive observers, or that they were, if not charlatans, designing politicians deliberately riding a false issue into office. The most charitable interpretation to be put upon the course of the Republicans is that they did not realize what they were doing, that they were carelessly playing with fire. Now if we know anything, it is that Abraham Lincoln was not a fool. And we know, too, that while Lincoln was a politician, superbly skilled and certainly ambitious, he was one with a high degree of principle. To say that he did not understand what was happening or that he understood and did not consider the results simply does not make sense. We must look for another explanation.

We will never comprehend the events of the 1850's if we insist on looking at them through our eyes. That decade, like every other period, is a living, vibrant page of history, and while we may admit that sometimes men act from motives of which they are unaware, still we must try to see the motives they thought they had. How, then, did things appear to Lincoln and other Republicans in those years? They saw a sequence of happenings that disturbed them, and they came to a conclusion, which if not inevitable, was certainly natural for them to reach. The Compromise of 1850, coming after a dangerous crisis, had seemed to settle finally the sectional controversy. Then four years later the Kansas-Nebraska Act, apparently but not actually an expression of southern aggression, *seemed* to open new territory to slavery. Then the Dred Scott decision was announced, hitting the Republicans like a bombshell. The broad tenor of the decision is well-known, but the implications in some of the opinions have not been adequately analyzed and it was these implications that troubled the Republicans and notably Lincoln. It was not just that the Supreme Court said Congress could not exclude slavery from the territories, bad as that was. Chief Justice Taney and Justice Nelson, whether or not they meant to, seemed to go much farther. They said that the right to property in slaves was "expressly affirmed" in the Constitution.

That is, slavery had a special and specific sanctity not attached to other forms of property.

This was the part of the decision that aroused Lincoln, that led him to charge that there was a deliberate plan to extend slavery. For if slavery was expressly protected by the Constitution, could a state, even a state where it did not exist, bar it? Would not some future decision open all the states to slavery? We think that Lincoln read more into the decision than was there, but was his reaction without reason? One other feature of the case deserves notice. Professor Harry Jaffa has said that the Dred Scott decision was a summons to the Republican party to disband. If it was not quite that, it was a judicial declaration that the platform of a major party was unconstitutional. On several occasions in our history the Supreme Court has placed itself in a position where it seemed to be thwarting the will of a large proportion of the people, but seldom if ever has it done so as starkly as in 1857. Is it then so surprising that Lincoln thought there was something queer afoot? Or that he denounced the decision as a blow at popular government?

It is evident that a real issue, or set of related issues, divided the American people in the 1850's. Whatever this issue was, it was not settled by the normal political democratic procedure but by a resort to force. Avery Craven has argued that the failure to find a peaceable solution represented a breakdown in the democratic process. Picturing the sectional conflict as revolving around issues cast in moral form and having to do with the fundamental structure of society, Craven suggests that democracy cannot solve issues that are really momentous. He quotes Carl Becker on the limitations of popular government. Becker said that "government by discussion works best when there is nothing of profound importance to discuss, and when there is plenty of time to discuss it. The party system works best when the rival programs involve the superficial aspects rather than the fundamental structure of the social system, and majority rule works best when the minority can meet defeat at the polls in good temper because they need not regard the decision as either a permanent or a fatal surrender of their vital interests."

Becker's dictum, not exactly original with him, was generally sound, although perhaps stated a little too cynically. The true function of parties in a democracy such as ours is to blunt differences, not to sharpen them. The true function of a democratic politician is to reconcile conflicting interests, not to push through a unitary interest. Nearly always our parties and politicians have been marvellously successful in doing their job. Only once have they been unable to bring it off—in the sectional crisis that eventuated so tragically in 1860-61. Inevitably we ask why there was a failure then? Why did the minority refuse to accept the will of the majority? Why did the majority refuse to compromise its position? The answer seems inescapable. The one great failure came over the one great issue that apparently we cannot settle by the ordinary political process— the race question, and it must always be stressed that slavery was a part of the larger race question. The race issue releases strange and flaming emotions that are alien to the democratic framework. When men are moved by these emotions, as the history of the 1850's and the 1950's attests, they are not easily satisfied with mere political discussion or readily susceptible to conventional political compromise. The slavery issue stirred passionate emotions in the North and the South. If it was not in itself a moral question, it aroused deep moral feelings in both attackers and defenders. And it became entangled with what is undoubtedly the most dynamic element in the American ethic, the principle of equality.

By the 1850's the controversy over slavery had reached a point where some kind of settlement had to be made. The issue was too big, too dangerous to be put off. Either the majority North had to be satisfied that a way would be found to get rid of slavery, preferably a way satisfactory to the South, or the North had to admit that slavery was a permanent institution on the American scene and stop attacking it. The latter probability was so unlikely that it may be dismissed. There remained the possibility that the North and the South could devise some solution acceptable to both. This was exactly what Lincoln was trying to do when he proposed his plan to bring about the destruction of slavery by excluding it from the territories. If slavery was penned up in the South, he thought, it would eventually disappear. His policy would, he liked to say, place slavery in such a condition as to bring about its ultimate extinction. Lincoln always stressed the word ultimate in discussing the end of slavery. The process he recommended would take years to complete; it was a kind of patient emancipation. But it was, and this is sometimes forgotten by critics, a fundamental solution. Finally there would be no slavery in America. Lincoln hoped that his plan would satisfy both sections.

Lincoln's solution was not adopted, nor was any plan to resolve the crisis put in motion. The South was not prepared to offer a plan of its own that involved any yielding on the question of race relationships. Professor Allan Nevins has criticized southern leaders for not nerving their people to pay the necessary price of race adjustment. But even if the leaders had favored some kind of compromise, they would not have dared to propose it—for the simple reason that the people would not hear of it. Perhaps the greatest tragedy of the sectional controversy is that the South could not proffer a solution. Of northern opinion we cannot speak with much certainty. We do not know if the North would have waited patiently for the South to change its attitude or if the North would have been satisfied with some gradual plan like Lincoln's; shortly the whole question would become academic. Humans cannot always control history, and when they do not history may determine its own course. By 1860 the situation was well out of the power of the American people to decide. Then only one resolution was possible. As Lincoln aptly put it: "And the war came."

Many elements went into the making of the Civil War—economic, political, social, and psychological. It is doubtless true that extremists and orators, and inept men and selfish men helped to hasten the coming of the crisis. But it would have come without them. The American people resorted to the final arbitration for reasons that they considered real and important. What these reasons were historians will continue to argue as long as there are historians. Probably we will never be able to separate the various strands of the war's causation. But in evaluating their significance we would be wise to give some weight to the appraisal of the greatest judge of popular opinion that this country has seen. Abraham Lincoln said during the war that slavery had always been the disturbing element in the national house. And again he said: "Without the institution of slavery, and the colored race as a basis, the war could not have an existence."

ROBERT M. SUTTON

Lincoln and

The Railroads of Illinois

"This is, indeed, a very desirable object. No other improvement that reason will justify us in hoping for, can equal in utility the rail road." (Communication to the People of Sangamon County, March 9, 1832)

Abraham Lincoln in an almost literal sense grew up with American railroads. The three decades of his public career coincide in a remarkable way with the first great surge of railroad building in this country which was arrested by the Panic of 1857 and brought to a temporary halt by the Civil War. During those years railroad mileage in the United States increased from twenty-three in 1830 to more than 30,000 in 1860. For Illinois the figure was equally spectacular, growing from no rail mileage at all in the earlier year to nearly 3,000 miles on the eve of the war. In addition to being an interested spectator concerned with all phases of the great "transportation revolution" during these years, Lincoln was on many occasions an active participant in the rapidly unfolding drama. In his adopted state of Illinois where this participation was most extensive Lincoln gave much attention and direction to, and was greatly influenced by, the course of railroad development and expansion. First as a state legislator, later as an attorney for a number of Illinois lines, and finally as Chief Executive of the nation he figured prominently in many aspects of this new mode of transportation.

Not long after he had taken up residence at New Salem and in the course of his first election campaign (1832) Lincoln revealed his interest in the potentialities of the "iron horse." Taking note of a meeting of Morgan County citizens who were inquiring into the feasibility of a railroad to run from the Illinois River to Springfield via Jacksonville, Lincoln commented, "This is, indeed, a very desirable object. No other improvement that reason will justify us in hoping for, can equal in utility

41

the rail road." Though he found the cost of this proposed line (estimated at $290,000) to be excessive and recommended instead the improvement of the Sangamon River, the above quotation represents a point of view which Lincoln seems never to have seriously questioned throughout the remainder of his public career.

One of the major and continuing concerns of Illinois during the early years of statehood was with internal improvements. Basically, the question was how best to improve the state's internal transportation facilities in order to encourage additional settlement and further stimulate trade and commerce. Particularly pressing was the problem of how to market the growing output of an increasing population predominantly engaged in agriculture. Many plans for the improvement of rivers and the construction of turnpikes, railroads, and canals were advanced in the General Assembly before 1836, and in most instances charters were granted to individuals or groups giving them authority to proceed with their individual projects. Almost nothing was accomplished along this line, however, since the resources available to the promoter were generally insufficient to the task before him.

Finally, however, a number of the more likely projects were brought together in an omnibus internal improvements measure laid before the General Assembly during the 1836-37 session. "An Act to Establish and Maintain a General System of Internal Improvements for the state of Illinois" had it been realized in its entirety would have revolutionized state transportation. In addition to the highly thought of Illinois and Michigan Canal which had been authorized by the previous Legislature, this act committed the state to a series of river and road improvements and to an unbelievably ambitious program of railroad building calling for more than 1,300 miles of lines. The main stem or trunk of the system, called the Central Railroad, would run through the heart of the state from the southern tip at or near Cairo to a point in the extreme northwest around Galena. A number of cross-state lines were planned to intersect the trunk at several points, and also to perform the additional function of tying together, laterally, the three main rivers which were so essential to the trade and commerce of early Illinois—the Mississippi, the Illinois, and the Wabash-Ohio.

Because of the reckless and ill-conceived character of the internal improvements drive, Lincoln scholars have been somewhat embarrassed by the prominent roll which the young Whig legislator from Sangamon County played in it. Having apparently overcome his earlier antipathy for the sizeable expenditure of public funds, Lincoln and his colleagues obligated the state of Illinois for appropriations totaling more than ten million dollars. Nicolay and Hay remark, "If Mr. Lincoln had no other claim to be remembered than his services in the Legislature of 1836-37, there would be little to say in his favor. . . . The most we can say for Mr. Lincoln is that he obeyed the will of his constituents, as he promised to do, and labored with singular skill and ability to accomplish the objects desired by the people who gave him their votes." Lincoln's law partner of later years, William H. Herndon, concluded a lengthy criticism of the Legislature with these words: "However much we may regret that Lincoln took part and aided in this reckless legislation, we must not forget that his party and all his constituents gave him their united endorsement."

Though there may be some basis for a difference of opinion about the degree of leadership which Lincoln exercised with respect to the internal improvements matter, there is no question but that he gave his constant and vigorous support to it. Whatever basis for disagreement there is arises out of the question of the relative importance which he and his colleagues from Sangamon County (the famous "Long Nine") attached to the internal improvement measure in comparison with that which they gave to another issue also before the 10th General Assembly. It should be borne in mind that the question of the relocation of the state capital, then at Vandalia, was also under consideration, and Springfield was one of the strong candidates for the honor. "Log rolling" and vote trading are not novelties to the Illinois General Assembly and contemporary observers were convinced that the legislative session of 1836-37 had set new records for such practices. In the end, Springfield became the new state capital and the improvements measure became law over the suspensive veto of the awkward Council of Revision, as provided for in the Illinois Constitution of 1818.

The economic history of Illinois is dominated for the next decade by the specter of internal improvements. Her near-frenzied efforts to carry out the various projects included in the system appear to have been generated by a kind of haunting fear that otherwise progress might very well pass her by—progress, of course, measured in terms of population, industry, commerce, and wealth.

Beset with faulty planning from the outset, the almost total failure of the Act is scarcely more attributable to inexperience, inadequate financing, and short-sighted execution than it is to a colossal misfortune in timing which saw the launching of the program occur almost simultaneously with the onset of the Panic of 1837. When all construction was necessarily halted in 1840, Illinois could boast of twenty-four miles of completed railroad on the Northern Cross line between Meredosia and Jacksonville and a state debt of over $14,000,000.

The lessons of failure were dearly learned. Illinois struggled for years with a heritage of debt which brought her to the threshold of repudiation in the dark days of the 1840's. Solon Robinson, Indiana agriculturalist and farm editor, upon visiting central Illinois in 1845, described the state's only operating railroad as, "another of the links of that endless chain that was to bind the state in love together, but has bound them in debt forever. It is already so dilapidated that mules have been substituted for locomotives, and as it fails to pay expenses, it must shortly go out of use for want of repairs." Railroad building, when it finally did come to Illinois, came under the auspices of private capital and not as state-sponsored public works projects.

Only gradually was the state able to liquidate the havoc of panic and depression. Nevertheless, throughout this period of discouragement Abraham Lincoln's convictions about the necessity and value of internal improvements seem never to have wavered. Both during his years of service in the General Assembly and in his single inconspicuous term in Congress there was no point upon which he was any more consistent than in his support of this orthodox Whig view of internal improvements. Governor Thomas Ford (1842-46) who deserves great credit for leading Illinois out of the economic morass of the 1840's said of him: "Mr. Lincoln is continually found voting with his friends in favor of this [internal improvements] legislation, and there is nothing to show that he saw any danger in it. He was a Whig, and as such in favor of internal improvements in general and a liberal construction of constitutional law in such matters."

Lincoln's activities in behalf of railroads during the 1840's were of necessity carefully measured. Except for attendance at an occasional convention called to advertize the need for a certain public improvement (which usually culminated in a petition to Congress for a grant of public land in support of the project) there is little to report. His term as a representative in the Thirtieth Congress (1847-49) broadened his outlook substantially, while the previous unhappy experience of Illinois with state-sponsored works helps to account for his renewed interest in internal improvements at federal expense. In Congress he did all he could to secure grants of public land for Illinois, and presented numerous petitions and memorials on behalf of Illinois citizens for support of this kind. He was a consistent and vigorous defender of river and harbor legislation which could scarcely fail to benefit Illinois, and he championed unsuccessfully a measure which would have given Illinois and other western states the same amount of public land in support of railroad construction as had been given to Ohio. Very little success attended any of these moves, however, and the repeated efforts of Sidney Breese and Stephen A. Douglas to secure public land for the Central Railroad project suffered the same fate. Nevertheless, their leadership in the Senate and the support of Lincoln and the Illinois delegation in the House went far toward keeping this dream alive and before Congress until it could be realized.

The year 1848 represents the beginning of a new era in Illinois transportation. The opening of the Illinois and Michigan Canal in April and the completion of the first segment of the Galena and Chicago Union Railroad in October of that year signal the end of the long period of depression and inertia which sobered the state after the 1837 intoxication. These events also form a backdrop for the most significant decade in Illinois railroad history. When, under Senator Douglas' leadership, the first federal land grant in support of railroad construction became law on September 20, 1850, the Prairie State had just over 100 miles of railroad in operation. At the close of the decade the total was approaching 3,000 and Illinois stood second among the American states in total railroad mileage. The handsome grant of public land to the states of Illinois, Mississippi and Alabama not only called into being the Illinois Central Railroad and resuscitated the expiring Mobile and Ohio project, but it also provided a tremendous stimulus to railroad building throughout the west on the part of private companies.

Furthermore, the success of the Douglas-sponsored land grant measure with its dream of a "Lakes to Gulf" rail connection was due in large part to the fact that an attempt had at last been made to develop a line of truly national consequence. The decision by Stephen A. Douglas to join forces with the South in seeking such support is a mark of his developing political astuteness, and stands in sharp contrast to the earlier failures of Illinois congressmen and senators (including both Douglas and Lincoln) to secure public support for a railroad contained entirely within the boundaries of Illinois.

The Illinois Central was the only one of the railroads of this state to receive land grant support, thus its origin and development are unique in the history of Illinois. Chartered by the General Assembly of the state of Illinois on February 10, 1851, and entrusted with the federal land grant of approximately 2,595,000 acres, the railroad was required by its charter to satisfy the state on a number of points. A group of eastern capitalists headed by Robert Rantoul, Jr. of Massachusetts received the charter and agreed to construct the line according to certain specifications, to do it within a definite period of time, and, in return for the federal land grant, to pay a percentage of its gross earnings into the state treasury semi-annually.

The bulding of the Illinois Central Railroad between 1852 and 1856 was a truly magnificent achievement in a decade of great change. It was described upon its completion as one of the best built railroads in the West and as good as most of the eastern lines. Its 705 miles of main line track and branches marked it as the longest railroad in the country for that day. There would seem to be little question but that its builders had lived up to their charter obligation to construct a railroad "equal, in all respects, to the road leading from Boston to Albany . . . with such improvements as experience shall have shown to be expedient." The signs were unmistakable that Illinois was in the process of extricating herself from the effects of her earlier folly. The railroads which she had so desperately sought came fifteen years later than she had looked for them, but the material progress they brought far outran the fondest dreams of 1837.

In the pattern of a rapidly developing state, Lincoln, the lawyer, found new outlets for his restless ambition. In connection with his short-lived congressional term he had experienced a series of failures and frustrations which appeared likely to change the direction of his career. The unpopularity of his anti-war position and his sharp criticism of President Polk's Mexican War policy proved to be detrimental to him personally and embarrassing to the Whig party in Illinois. Biographers of Lincoln are in general agreement that for the next several years he virtually turned his back upon politics, but considering the low estate of his political fortunes it would perhaps be equally true to say that politics turned its back upon him for these years!

With no apparent future in politics and with his responsibilities increasing with the size of his family (William Wallace, the Lincolns' third son, was born in 1850), Lincoln turned with renewed enthusiasm to the practice of law. The coming of the railroads not only brought new business to the state of Illinois, but also brought a new type of business to the attorneys of the state. A great variety of cases involving personal injury, trespass, right-of-way, injury to livestock, property damage, suits concerning assessment on stock, freight claims, etc., appear during the 1850's; and there were, of course, appeals and countersuits arising from any and all of the above.

In terms of what was taking place in Illinois, Lincoln's role at the outset was not greatly different from that of a number of equally ambitious attorneys in this state and others. By the end of the decade, however, he had outstripped most of his fellows in the field of railroad law, and was one of the most successful, if not the most successful, corporation lawyer in the state of Illinois. As his law practice grew and became increasingly lucrative no single class of clients appeared on his accounts more often than did the railroads of Illinois. Furthermore, some of his most handsome fees came from these same railroads. At one time or another during the 1850's Lincoln appeared in cases involving the Atlantic and Mississippi (part of today's Pennsylvania System); Alton and Sangamon (Gulf, Mobile and Ohio); Chicago, Burlington and Quincy; Chicago and Rock Island; Great Western of Illinois (Wabash); Terre Haute and Alton (New York Central); and Tonica and Petersburg Railroads. In his earliest recorded cases Lincoln represented the Alton and Sangamon Railroad, and there is even some evidence that he was in the regular retainer of that company during 1851-52. By far his greatest service as a railroad attorney, however, was performed in the interest of the Illinois Central Railroad, and, except for his years of public service, Lincoln spent more time in the employ of the Illinois Central than in that of any other client.

Lincoln's earliest legal services for the Illinois Central are completely shrouded in mystery and thus often involved in controversy. There is no trustworthy record to indicate whether Lincoln supported or opposed the Rantoul group's proposal before the General Assembly in 1851 for a charter that would incorporate the transfer of the federal land grant into the company's hands. Neither is there any assurance that he was or was not the highly recommended but unnamed lobbyist mentioned in the correspondence of early company officials.

No uncertainty, however, surrounds his employment by the railroad from 1853 until the eve of his nomination for the presidency in 1860. During these years Lincoln represented the Illinois Central Railroad on many occasions and in a great variety of cases. Most of these were heard before the courts of the Eighth Judicial District in central Illinois, and at least eleven were carried to the Illinois Supreme Court. His first case of record for this railroad was a right-of-way matter tried in Bloomington before Circuit Judge David Davis on April 16, 1853. A similar case involving condemnation of a right-of-way was heard in Champaign County in May of the same year. More often than not, in cases of this sort, Lincoln was associated with various local attorneys for the company, such as Asahel Gridley in McLean County, Clifton H. Moore in DeWitt County, and Henry C. Whitney in Champaign County.

The tenuous and almost haphazard nature of the arrangement linking Lincoln with the Illinois Central is aptly described in the Lincoln correspondence of these years. On September 23, 1854, he wrote Mason Brayman, solicitor for the railroad, that he was drawing on the company for $100.

. . . The reason I have taken this liberty is, that since last fall, by your request I have declined all new business against the road, and out of which I suppose I could have realized several hundred dollars; have attended, both at De Witt and here [Bloomington] to a great variety of little business for the Co, most of which, however, remains unfinished, and have received nothing. I wish now to be charged with this sum, to be taken into account on settlement.

It is likely that the "great variety of little business" referred to here included the previously mentioned property damage, livestock injury, trespass, right-of-way, and condemnation suits. Almost a year later, on September 14, 1855, Lincoln wrote to James F. Joy, one of the foremost legal minds in the Middle West and at that time General Counsel of the Illinois Central:

I have to day drawn on you in favor of the McLean County Bank . . . for one hundred and fifty dollars. This is intended as a fee for all services done by me for the Illinois Central Railroad, since last September, within the counties of McLean and De Witt. Within that term . . . I have assisted, for the Road, in at least fifteen cases (I believe, one or two more) and I have concluded to lump them off at ten dollars a case. . . .

Lincoln continued to be available for legal employment of this sort throughout the remainder of the 1850's. As time went on, however, the simple damage and trespass-type cases gave way to issues which raised much more serious and sophisticated questions of law.

One of the finest examples of this type of litigation and certainly the best known case which Lincoln handled for the Illinois Central is properly described as the *Illinois Central Railroad Company vs. the County of McLean and George Parke, Sheriff and Collector,* but is more commonly known as the McLean County Tax Case. The unique provision in the company charter by which the railroad agreed to pay into the state treasury a percentage of its gross earnings in lieu of other taxes constitutes the heart of the case. Furthermore, the charter also provided that the property of the company would be exempt from all taxation for a period of six years. Given the meager sources of tax revenue which were available to local governmental units in those years it is no wonder that the counties and municipalities through which the Illinois Central was being built looked upon it with hungry eyes. Following the lead of McLean County they were determined to challenge not only the exclusive state tax feature of the charter, but the six-year moratorium on general taxes as well. In August, 1853, McLean County began proceedings to force the railroad to pay taxes on the property it owned within the county. The company refused to pay and brought suit in the McLean County Circuit Court to enjoin the collection of such taxes.

Lincoln was already involved in the question but from a somewhat different angle. It is clear from the record that he had already discussed with T. R. Webber, clerk of the Circuit Court, the possibility of such a suit on the part of Champaign County, for he wrote to Mr. Webber, on September 12, 1853, apparently soon after Mason Brayman sought to engage him as counsel for the company:

> . . . An effort is about to be made to get the question of the right to so tax the Co. before the court, & ultimately before the Supreme Court, and the Co. are offering to engage me for them. As this will be the same question I have had under consideration for you, I am somewhat trammelled by what has passed between you and me; feeling that you have the prior right to my services; if you choose to secure me a fee something near such as I can get from the other side. The question, in its magnitude, to the Co. on the one hand, and the counties in which the Co. has land, on the other, is the largest law question that can now be got up in the State; and therefore, in justice to myself, I can not afford, if I can help it, to miss a fee altogether. If you choose to release me; say so by return mail, and there an end. If you wish to retain me, you better get authority from your court, come directly over [to Bloomington] in the Stage and make common cause with this county.

For the moment it appeared quite likely that Champaign County would retain his services. County Judge J. B. Thomas recommended the employment of Lincoln and urged Webber to go immediately to Bloomington prepared to offer a fee "in proportion to the importance of the claim," even up to $500 if necessary. However, for some unknown reason the negotiations fell through, and on October 3, 1853, Lincoln wrote to Attorney Brayman, "Neither the county of McLean nor any one on it's behalf, has yet made any engagement with me in relation to it's suit with the Illinois Central Railroad, on the subject of taxation. I am now free to make an engagement for the Road; and if you think fit you may 'count me in' . . ."

The company moved quickly to engage him, and Brayman forwarded (on October 7) a check for $250, saying in his letter that it was to be considered a general retainer, "other charges to be adjusted between us as the character of the business in which you may be called upon to engage may render proper." Apparently the Illinois Central did not relish the idea of facing Lincoln as counsel for the opposition in this or any similar situation, and the only sure way of preventing such an eventuality was to engage him on a semi-permanent basis. In due course of time the tax case was argued at the fall term of the McLean County Circuit Court, was decided against the company, and an appeal was taken to the Illinois Supreme Court. It appears that there was no real contest in the Circuit Court, as it was generally understood that the Supreme Court would be called upon to make the final decision. The court's decree granting the appeal contained the stipulation that the only question to be raised in the Supreme Court was whether or not the road could be taxed by a county authority.

The potentialities of this case were enormous. For the railroad an adverse decision could very well have had fatal consequences. It was no secret that if McLean County were successful in its suit, every one of the counties through which the Illinois Central Railroad ran would institute similar cases at the earliest possible moment. Therefore, should the court decide that local taxes could be levied in addition to the charter tax figure due the state, the railroad would almost certainly have been crushed under an intolerable tax burden. This would have been particularly difficult during the early years of operation when revenues often exceeded expenditures by a very narrow margin.

Those who have written from the company's point of view have often argued that a decision against the railroad and in favor of McLean County might well have been a blessing in disguise. If by this they mean that the state tax would have been declared invalid, and regular local taxation substituted for it, there is a degree of merit in their contention. It is by no means as simple as this, however, for what they fail to take into account is that if sections 18 and 22 of the company's charter could be overturned in court so might other features and sections be similarly attacked and invalidated. Given the growing antimonopoly spirit present in Illinois of the 1850's (which found its fullest expression in the Granger movement twenty years later) it was not probable that the Illinois Central would be readily released from the requirements of the 1851 charter. It seems far more likely that in view of the highly prized and much sought after land grant the state would insist upon either a vigorous enforcement or a drastic reappraisal of the company's responsibilities under the charter.

In the Supreme Court the case was argued early in 1854 by Lincoln and James F. Joy for the railroad, and by Stephen T. Logan and John T. Stuart, both former law partners of Lincoln, for McLean County. The court was in such doubt, however, that the case was continued and a rehearing was ordered so that "full discussion and deliberate examination might remove these apparent difficulties." Nearly two years later, on January 16-17, 1856, the case was heard again, with Lincoln making the opening argument and Joy concluding for the railroad. Counsel for the company (probably Lincoln because of his acquaintance with the Illinois legal and constitutional system) made the point that the real issue was not between McLean County and the Illinois Central Railroad, but between the county and the state of Illinois, since the action of the county in attempting to tax the road under the general laws of the constitutional rule of uniformity in matters of taxation was in direct conflict with the railroad's charter granted by the General Assembly.

The Supreme Court evidently gave considerable weight to this argument, and, in a long and tediously involved opinion, held unanimously that under the Illinois Constitution the Legislature could make exceptions from the rule of uniformity, that the provision in the company's charter requiring payment to the state of a percentage of its gross earnings represented such an exception, and that counties, therefore, could not tax the road. The decision of the McLean County Circuit Court was, accordingly, reversed.

For the Illinois Central the favorable decision in the tax case provided the company with a temporary degree of security at a critical period in its history. Coming into full operation late in 1856, its dreams of profits and prosperity were completely shattered a year later by the Panic of 1857, and it, in company with numerous other American railroads, struggled through the remainder of the decade under depressed circumstances.

When he was finally forced to sue to collect what the company must have considered an excessively high fee for services rendered ($5,000), Lincoln probably felt that his usefulness to the Illinois Central was at an end. Early in 1857 a firm of attorneys in Paris, Illinois, approached him about handling a claim against the Illinois Central. Lincoln replied, "I have been in the regular retainer of the Co. for two or three years; but I expect they do not wish to retain me any longer. . . . I am going to Chicago, . . . on the 21st. Inst. and I will then ascertain whether they [will] discharge me; & if they do, as I expect, I will attend to your business & write you. . . ."

Following a conference with company officials in Chicago, and much to his surprise, the railroad continued him in their employ and apparently agreed to enter no vigorous defense in his impending fee suit growing out of the McLean County matter. In passing it might be said that instead of taking the case proffered by the Paris attorneys, Lincoln along with Orlando Ficklin of Charleston defended the Illinois Central before the Supreme Court. The main issue in this case concerned the responsibility of the railroad for livestock shipped over its line and was decided in the company's favor, thus establishing the right of a railroad to restrict its liability as a common carrier.

The company's motives in continuing to retain Lincoln on their legal staff are clearly evident from a letter written by Ebenezer Lane, resident director of the railroad in Chicago and a former Chief Justice of the Supreme Court of Ohio, to William H. Osborn, president of the Illinois Central Railroad whose office was then in New York.

> . . . We can now look back and in some degree estimate the narrow escape we have made (I hope and believe entirely) from burdens of the most serious character. While Lincoln was prosecuting his lawsuit for fees, it was natural for him to expect a dismissal from the Company's service and being a politician aspiring to the Senate, to entertain plans of making an attack upon the company not only in a revengeful spirit, but as subservient to his future advancement. . . . He kept this to himself, but before our settlement with him, the

Auditor [Jesse K. Dubois] a vain, self-sufficient but weak man, approached him with a view to retain him for the State for consultation. Lincoln answered he was not free from his engagement to us, but expected a discharge. . . .

Meanwhile we settled with Lincoln and fortunately took him out of the field, or rather engaged him for our interests. This is the more fortunate as he proves to be not only the most prominent of his political party, but the acknowledged special adviser of the Bissell administration. . . .

It is fairly evident then that some time before the much-discussed fee trial in June, 1857, the company had determined to pay Lincoln his large fee, and that their primary purpose in doing so was to be certain of obtaining his services in connection with anticipated difficulties involving the State Auditor and concerning the levying and assessment of the state tax.

This new series of cases, while much less well known than the McLean County tax case, is certainly its equal in every respect. Once again the fate of the company hung in the balance as the state of Illinois prepared to go to court in an effort to further determine the extent of its tax privileges under sections 18 and 22 of the railroad's charter. There are those who believe this to be Lincoln's supreme legal achievement on behalf of the Illinois Central Railroad. Considering the complexities of the case, the absence of legal precedents, the critical state of the company's finances, and its repercussions in the General Assembly (including even the whisper of bribery and corruption in that body) such a view is entirely justified.

Charles Leroy Brown ably summarized the whole affair some years ago in the pages of the *Journal of the Illinois State Historical Society.*

> The new work for which Lincoln was thus engaged in 1857 was of extreme delicacy. Lincoln proceeded slowly on a program of strategy, maneuver and conciliation which involved, among other things, the enactment of an extraordinary statute [by the state legislature]. Then followed two important original actions tried in the Supreme Court of Illinois. In those cases the evidence of many witnesses was introduced before the Supreme Court sitting as a trier of facts. Lincoln won both cases. The court proceedings escaped the attention of the newspapers of the time. In one of these two cases the Supreme Court rendered no opinion but entered a judgment of vital importance to the company. In the other the Supreme Court filed a long

opinion highly favorable to the railroad. That opinion was rendered in March, 1860, at the January, 1860, term, but it was not published in the reports with other opinions rendered at the same term; it was not published until 1863. And when published in the printed volume of the reports many pages of the opinion as it appears in the formal opinion record of the court were omitted.

This complex business occupied the attention of Lincoln from time to time over a period of nearly three years. The outcome rested mainly on the answers to three questions: one, what was the true evaluation of Illinois Central property; two, should the company's property be valued on the same basis for tax purposes as that of other railroads in Illinois; three, could the gross income tax of 5%, as provided in section 18 of the state charter, plus the state tax, mentioned in section 22, exceed a figure equal to 7% of the company's gross revenues? Thanks to the favorable rulings by the Illinois Supreme Court and with an assist from the General Assembly, the Illinois Central was able to set the valuation on its property at such a figure that it would be liable for no additional state taxes beyond the minimum 7% of gross revenues—about which liability there was no question. Brown believes that the decision rescued the company from foreclosure and financial collapse. The expressions of relief voiced by company officials certainly lend weight to this viewpoint. Resident Director Lane's words would have been equally appropriate at this point: "We can now look back and in some degree estimate the narrow escape we have made . . . from burdens of the most serious character."

Following the Supreme Court's decision in March, 1860, Lincoln appeared in still another case in which the Illinois Central was indirectly interested. The so-called "Sand Bar Case" (*Johnson vs. Jones and Marsh*) was heard in Federal District Court during April. Since this was only a month prior to the meeting of the Republican National Convention at the "Wigwam" in Chicago, it is likely that he spent every available spare moment meeting influential friends, developing strategy, and building "political fences" in his drive for the Republican presidential nomination.

The conspicuous success which Lincoln appeared to be having as counsel for the Illinois Central brought an increasing number of railroad clients to his door. During the time that the tax case was before the Su-

55

preme Court (1854-56) Lincoln handled additional cases for the Illinois Central, as well as for the Chicago, Alton and St. Louis, Chicago and Rock Island, Terre Haute and Alton, and the Ohio and Mississsippi, all significant lines in the transportation history of pre-Civil War Illinois. In this same period he played a major role in back-stage efforts to block the ambitions of the Indiana-sponsored Mississippi and Atlantic Railroad (also known as the Terre Haute and Illinoistown) whose competition was feared by both the Ohio and Mississippi and the Terre Haute and Alton. Finally, he represented individual clients in suits involving the Great Western Railroad (of Illinois) and the Chicago, Burlington and Quincy.

A matter which arose in 1857 illustrates not only the new eminence held by Lincoln among the members of the Illinois bar, but also his widening interest in larger and more fundamental issues of national transportation. Employing a subsidiary corporation, the Chicago and Rock Island Railroad Company built and opened for business on April 21, 1856, the first bridge across the Mississippi River between Rock Island, Illinois, and Davenport, Iowa. Two weeks later (on May 6) the steamer *Effie Afton,* owned by St. Louis shipping interests, went out of control while passing the bridge on its way upstream, collided with one of the piers and was thrown against another resulting in a fire which destroyed the vessel and seriously damaged the bridge.

Captain Hurd and other owners of the boat immediately brought suit against the bridge company, alleging that the *Effie Afton* was carefully and skilfully navigated at the time of the accident, and that the boat "was forcibly driven by the currents and eddies caused by said piers against one of them," with the aforementioned results. The plaintiff's argument concluded that the bridge was a serious and permanent obstruction to navigation and damages were sought to the value of the boat and cargo, with insurance. The defendants, of course, denied the charges; "and this," said Justice John McLean in his instructions to the jury, "is the important issue you are sworn to try."

The contest was far more than a simple damage suit. In reality, it was a trial of strength between St. Louis and other cities and towns on the Mississippi and Ohio Rivers on the one hand, and Chicago and similar inland railroad centers on the other. Prior to the 1850's, the Mississippi River and its tributaries provided the main artery for trade and commerce in the western states and territories. With the gradual development of railroads centering upon Chicago (and to a lesser degree upon St. Louis) the predominantly east-west flow of railborn commerce provided a new and serious form of competition for the traditionally north-south oriented river trade.

Hurd et al vs. Railroad Bridge Company brought this issue into sharp focus and revealed something of the antagonism which characterized the conflict between river boat interests and railroad promoters. "The Railroad Bridge at Rock Island is an intolerable nuisance," thundered the *St. Louis Republican.* ". . . It is utterly impossible for any man not an idiot to note the disasters at Rock Island and honestly ascribe them to any other cause than the huge obstruction to navigation which the Bridge Company have built there and insist shall remain even though lives by the score and property by the millions are destroyed every year." The *Chicago Tribune* was slightly more restrained when it declared in an editorial, "Facts . . . do not warrant the incessant clamor kept up by those who insist that that magnificent and necessary structure shall be torn down. We trust that . . . the outcries of the St. Louis and river press may be silenced."

Associated with Norman B. Judd of Chicago and Joseph Knox of Rock Island, Lincoln appears to have occupied the key role in the strategy of defense. He had prepared meticulously for the case by visiting Rock Island in advance of the court term where he gathered his evidence with great care by examining the bridge, noting the speed and direction of the river currents and eddies in relation to the bridge piers, and even having a model of the *Effie Afton* built which he would use in the courtroom. After the trial, heard before the Federal District Court in Chicago, had run its course, Lincoln made the closing speech for the Bridge Company. In essence, his argument was that the Mississippi, "extending almost from where it never freezes to where it never thaws" was the great waterway for the commerce of the valley, and to block it was unthinkable. Nevertheless, its interest was no greater than the demands of travel and traffic from east to west. The westward flow of settlement was cited as "building up new countries with a rapidity never before seen in the history of the world." Occupying portions of two days, he made an elaborate examination of the evidence, and in conclusion reminded the jury that the burden of proof was upon the plaintiff to show that the bridge was a "material obstruction and that they have managed their boat with reasonable care and skill." Following closing arguments by counsel for the plaintiff, Judge McLean gave the charge to the jury, which then retired to deliberate the matter. Later in the evening the jury announced that they were sharply divided and that there seemed to be no prospect of agreement, whereupon they were dismissed.

Though the circumstance of a "hung jury" is unsatisfactory and far from conclusive, it should not be allowed to obscure the fact that in this case the failure of the river interests to prove their contentions about the hazard and nuisance character of the bridge represented a significant victory for the westward moving railroads of the country. On the other hand, a total victory for the river interests would have been a calamity of the severest sort for rail promoters and would have resulted in at least a temporary setback for trans-Mississippi railroad building as well as a potential obstacle to western territorial development.

The bridge suit was subsequently reinstituted by the river interests in the courts of Iowa where they won a favorable decision. Upon appeal to the United States Supreme Court, however, the ruling of the Iowa court was reversed thus reaffirming the right of railroads to bridge navigable rivers, with just regard, of course, for the rights of water navigation. The Mississippi River Bridge Case and similar litigation in other parts of the country stand as prime examples of the new stature of railborn commerce and the concurrent decline of river trade in the decade preceding the Civil War.

If one were to ask to what extent the railroad interests of Abraham Lincoln and Stephen A. Douglas entered into the senatorial contest of 1858, the answer would have to be, only in a very minor and incidental sort of way. Except for an occasional reference by Lincoln to the favored treatment (special trains, private cars, and his specially equipped flat car with a twelve-pounder cannon attached) accorded Douglas during the canvass, and retaliatory thrusts on the part of Douglas to the effect that Lincoln had defrauded the state out of millions of dollars in tax money in return for a handsome fee from the Illinois Central, their railroad connections remain very much in the background. Lincoln appears to have been the more sensitive of the two, probably because he was the more vulnerable, and on several occasions he abandoned his usual line of attack to refute the allegations of Douglas. He was sufficiently concerned to devote a considerable portion of his remarks to this matter in a speech at Carthage, Illinois, on October 22, 1858, in which he very carefully reviewed his relationship with both the Illinois Central and the state in the McLean County tax case.

From another point of view the railroads of Illinois were absolutely essential to the planning and execution of the Lincoln-Douglas debates. This tense and colorful political drama was a tribute to the transportation revolution which had occurred in Illinois. Given the limited time available to the contestants and the distances involved in their effort to fully canvass the state, it would have been impossible to stage the debates on the scale on which we know them before 1857 or 1858. The late Harry E. Pratt, former state historian of Illinois, has pointed out that phenomenal railroad construction in the 1850's made it possible for Douglas to travel over 5,000 miles in 100 days, while Lincoln, in a slightly longer period of time, covered approximately 4,350 miles, of which some 350 were by boat, 600 by carriage, and 3,400 by train. In the brief period of two days, Lincoln left Vermont, Illinios, on October 27, traveling by carriage to Macomb (18 miles), where he boarded the Chicago, Burlington and Quincy Railroad for Chicago (225 miles); changing to the Chicago, Alton and St. Louis he returned to Springfield (200 miles), then by carriage to Petersburg (20 miles), where he spoke on October 29, 1858. Such movement and tight scheduling would have been out of the question five years earlier.

As the tempo of Lincoln's participation in state and national politics quickened toward the end of the decade, one might expect to find a corresponding dimunition in his legal activity. Such, however, does not appear to have been the case, and, as was previously pointed out, he was to be found representing clients in court until approximately a month before his nomination for the presidency. For nearly a decade he had followed and observed the dramatic changes which the railroad era had introduced into Illinois. Moreover, he had been more than a mere spectator of change; he was in fact a part of it and had left his personal imprint upon it. There can be no doubt that Lincoln's numerous services performed for Illinois railroads during the 1850's contributed to his training and conditioning for future leadership. The prestige that was his as a successful and much sought after attorney, the important contacts, personal and political, which he made in the course of his work, and his steadily increasing financial security growing out of the practice of law cannot be ignored. It will be argued (and immediately conceded) that none of these is as significant as his gradually assumed position as leader and spokesman for the moderate, free-soil, Republican party. But it should also be remembered that the event which went farthest toward establishing him as a national figure—his opportunity to challenge Douglas for the senatorship in 1858—was only possible because of his wide and favorable reputation in this state and the healthy condition of his personal finances, both of which were direct outgrowths of his extensive law practice.

Although Lincoln's close relationship with the railroads of Illinois comes to an end with the presidential election of November, 1860, his new and larger responsibilities constantly drew upon the Illinois experience. Whether it was applauding the audacious move of Governor Richard Yates in using a special troop train movement on the Illinois Central to occupy strategically-located Cairo, Illinois, on April 24, 1861, or signing an Act of Congress on January 31, 1862, authorizing the President to take possession of the railroads of the United States, if and when, in his judgment, the safety and welfare of the country demanded it, or whether it was the support he gave to the Pacific Railroad bill which became law on July 2, 1862, one gets the impression that Lincoln more than most of his wartime associates understood and appreciated the new factor which the railroad had introduced into war and conquest. At the outbreak of the Civil War the Union possessed a rail system vastly superior in both mileage and cohesiveness to that to be found in the South. The ultimate recognition and exploitation of that decided advantage is the basis for the conviction that, to a very considerable extent, "victory rode the rails." Of that victory there were many engineers, not the least of whom was the Chief Executive himself.

Lincoln and

Lyman Trumbull

I cannot conceive it possible for me to be a rival of yours, or to take sides against you in favor of a rival. (Lincoln to Trumbull, Springfield, February 3, 1859)

For a quarter of a century the careers of Lincoln and Lyman Trumbull crossed and recrossed like grapevines in the wildwood. Alternately Lincoln and Trumbull belabored and befriended each other through the politically tempestuous years. In a sense they were chips from the same political timber; in another sense they could not have been more different. They were both intelligently devoted believers in the common man and democracy. Good political infighters and master craftsmen of the law, they attracted a loyal circle of political followers. Lincoln, however, was a superior public speaker, and a master of the written language; whereas Trumbull, as both a speaker and a writer, had a style as dry as a legal brief and as undramatic as a salary check. In 1840, the first time their political paths crossed, the casual observer might have judged them to be promising young politicians without feeling that either was far superior to the other. In 1865 Lincoln by his tremendous growth had so far outstripped Trumbull, admittedly a very capable man, that no impartial observer could have doubted Lincoln's superiority.

Trumbull, like Lincoln, was not a native Illinoisan. He was born in Colchester, Conn., on October 12, 1813. Unlike Lincoln, Trumbull was born into a prominent family; hence his opportunities for education were much better than were Lincoln's. Yet since his children were numerous, Lyman's father, Yale-trained himself, could not afford to send his sons to his alma mater. Lyman Trumbull had to work on the family farm alternate terms after he grew older, but until he was eighteen he was able to

61

acquire a classical education at Bacon Academy, a place of learning in his home town, only a notch below Yale College. He learned to write and spell uncommonly well for that time, even though he never mastered an easy and graceful style.

When he was twenty, and after teaching school in the East, Trumbull sought wider horizons for his talents, and hearing that schoolmasters were in great demand in the South, he migrated there. After some search he found that teaching opportunities were not plentiful. Nevertheless, he obtained a position as principal at Greenville Academy, Greenville, Meriwether County, Georgia, where he taught for the next three years as a successful teacher-prinicpal. School teaching, since it provided leisure to study and read, was considered a way for poor-but-enterprising young men to get a start in the world, but the low salary hardly qualified it as a permanent profession. Always ambitious, Trumbull used his leisure moments to read law in the office of a judge of the Superior Court of Georgia.

In Georgia he always felt cut off from polite society and more tolerated than liked as a Yankee school teacher. He, having saved his money with all the parsimony of a nudge, left Georgia to practice his new profession in greener fields.

In the spring of 1837 Trumbull migrated to Illinois. Settling in Belleville he quickly exhibited promise and was selected as a junior law partner by a former Illinois governor, John Reynolds. Using Reynolds as an entree to Illinois politics, Trumbull soon became active in the Democratic party, whose ticket he had voted in Georgia.

Trumbull was ready to stump southern Illinois in behalf of President Martin Van Buren against the cause of the Whigs' William Henry Harrison, when the exciting log cabin campaign of 1840 claimed the attention of the nation. Lincoln, who had earlier joined the Illinois Whig party, as he had been selected as an elector, was active for Harrison in the campaign.

The active campaign by the Whigs, usually an easy to beat minority, worried the Democrats in Trumbull's home county, who ignoring party seniority, scoured the organization to build the strongest slate of candidates. Consequently, Trumbull was nominated for the lower house of the

Legislature. After a strenuous hard-hitting campaign in the election of August 3, 1840, Trumbull led all the legislative candidates from the county, Whig and dissident-faction Democrats alike, with 1,756 votes. It was a notable victory since nationally the tide ran hard for the Whigs, although the Democrats managed to hold their traditional stronghold, Illinois. Since Reynolds, Trumbull's partner, had been elected to Congress, their legal partnership was dissolved. Trumbull took his younger brother George as a junior partner and continued a very active law practice despite his new duties as a state representative.

At twenty-seven Trumbull was the youngest member in attendance at the special session of the Legislature which met in November, 1840. In and around Springfield at this time there was a galaxy of political luminaries holding various state offices seldom equaled in any state capital. In addition to Lincoln, already a veteran state legislator, there were Stephen A. Douglas, David Davis, Richard Yates, Edward D. Baker, Sidney Breese, James Shields, Orville H. Browning, and William A. Richardson.

The Legislature was faced by urgent problems. A crisis resulting from the Panic of 1837, which had adversely affected the state banks and the internal improvement, gripped the state. Almost every time a matter concerning the internal improvement system arose, Trumbull and Lincoln found themselves on the opposite sides of the debate and the voting. Lincoln was trying to ease the system out gracefully, and he viewed with disfavor Trumbull's root and branch opposition to it.

Lincoln's and Trumbull's careers crossed anew when staunch Whig Lincoln initiated an investigation of the high cost of printing charged the state by the Democrats. To quash Lincoln's charges peremptorily, two strong Democrats were appointed to the committee of investigation along with Lincoln himself. One of these Democrats, Lyman Trumbull, was named chairman. Lincoln attended every meeting of the committee, but he lacked his usual drive since this was January, 1841, and his personal life was in a turmoil because of his broken engagement with Mary Todd. As a result the committee was able to frame a report that was a complete vindication of the Democrats. Lincoln did not even issue a minority report.

Late in February, 1841, Governor Thomas Carlin appointed Trumbull as Douglas' successor as Secretary of State. At that time the Secretary of State's principal duty was keeping a record of the official acts of the Governor, and this required that the holder of the office be in the Governor's confidence. Trumbull was efficient in the routine of his office and so long as Carlin held the governorship all went well. However, Carlin's successor, Thomas Ford, elected in 1842, although he was also a Democrat, proved politically incompatible with Trumbull. He favored easy terms of liquidation for state banks while Trumbull was unwilling to grant them concessions. From his post as Secretary of State Trumbull led the unsuccessful opposition to the Governor's proposal. Irritated at what he regarded as treachery, Ford summarily removed him.

Nor was this the end. On March 3, 1843, the Illinois Legislature had appropriated $600.00 to enable the Secretary of State to construct marginal notes and an index to the state laws. The next day Trumbull had been removed from his post by Ford. However, Trumbull had anticipated this legislative authorization and had already completed two-thirds of the work. Consequently before leaving Springfield he had received from the State Auditor his compensation of $400.00 for the work already accomplished. Trumbull's successor as Secretary of State, Thompson Campbell, was furious when he learned of this and encouraged by Governor Ford he instituted a suit against Trumbull.

In his suit Campbell alleged that Trumbull had accomplished only one-third of the work and so had helped himself to a $200.00 overpayment. Although the incumbent Secretary won the first round in the Sangamon Circuit Court, the undaunted Trumbull appealed to the Illinois Supreme Court. As his attorney he retained Abraham Lincoln, whose fancy political footwork had impressed him and whose legal reputation was already secure. Lincoln as a Whig leader did not mind intervening in the intramural strife of the Democrats. On appeal the Supreme Court accepted lawyer Lincoln's contention that Campbell had no basis for an action against Trumbull.

While Trumbull had been Secretary of State he had met one of the town belles, Mary Todd, who was eventually to marry Lincoln. Almost forgotten is the fact that the flirtatious Mary, who had many beaux, was romantically interested in Trumbull for a short time. And so Trumbull and Lincoln were rivals in the drawing room as well as in the legislative halls and on the stump. Indeed, in June, 1841, Mary Todd wrote her good friend Mercy Levering referring to Trumbull as an "interesting gentleman" and continuing, "Now that your fortune is made, I feel much disposed in your absence, to lay *claims* as he [Trumbull] is talented and agreeable and sometimes *countenances* me."

The swirl of Springfield society seems to have drawn Trumbull and Mary Todd quickly apart. Mary enjoyed flirtations with Stephen Douglas and even the obscure Edwin B. Webb before Lincoln claimed her as a bride on November 4, 1842. By that time Lyman Trumbull was busily courting one of Mary's closest friends, Julia Jayne, whom he married on June 21, 1843, in the First Presbyterian Church in Springfield.

In the 1840's while Lincoln continued to take a prominent place in Whig party politics, until he was able successfully to claim a term as the congressman from the Springfield district, Trumbull found the time unrewarding after his removal as the Secretary of State. Governor Thomas Ford, who cordially hated Trumbull, determined to prevent his ever holding a public office again. As a result Ford threw the support of the "Springfield Clique" into the scales twice to defeat Trumbull's attempts to gain his district's congressional nomination. In 1846 Trumbull made a spirited try to obtain the gubernatorial nomination as Ford's successor, but the outgoing Governor was able to block Trumbull. Undeterred, Lyman Trumbull again sought the congressional nomination. This time by shrewd maneuvering he was able to defeat incumbent Robert Smith and gain the party endorsement. However Smith cried "fraud," and ran successfully as an independent with Whig support in the general election. Trumbull embarrassedly withdrew from active campaigning for two years, awash in the rough tides of politics.

If politically Trumbull's and Lincoln's paths had drawn apart, they remained socially acquainted since Trumbull's in-laws had a home in the Lincoln neighborhood. Since Trumbull's legal business often took him to Springfield, he brought his family along with him for extended visits, and as the years went by, Trumbull's eldest surviving son, Walter, became a playmate of Robert Todd Lincoln.

Meanwhile Trumbull's legal career had flourished. He appeared frequently before the Illinois Supreme Court, winning fifty-one of eighty-seven appeals or about sixty per cent of these cases. Appearing against the brightest legal lights in these cases he held his own with them all—excepting Abraham Lincoln. Lincoln won all three cases in which he appeared against Trumbull.

Through the encouragement of the then Governor Augustus C. French, Trumbull ran successfully in 1848 for a seat on the Illinois Supreme Court. He served four and a half years until 1853, but resigned despite his having won a new nine-year term in 1852, principally because the salary was inadequate to support his growing family. While he was on the bench, Trumbull saw a good deal of Lincoln, who enjoyed a wide practice before the Illinois Supreme Court.

After a severe bout of illness, Trumbull recovered his health in time to take an active part in the election of 1854. This election which split the old parties brought a new issue to the fore, the Kansas-Nebraska bill. Some Southerners gazed longingly at the lands west of Missouri and north of 36° 30′ where slavery had been banned since the Compromise of 1820. Their opportunity came when Illinois Senator Stephen A. Douglas fostered a bill in Congress to organize Kansas and Nebraska as territories. Realizing that he needed southern support for his measure, he revised it to provide for the repeal of the Missouri Compromise line and inserted a provision allowing the people living in these territories to decide for themselves whether or not they would have slavery. Making support of this bill a test of party loyalty, Douglas and the Franklin Pierce administration whipped up sufficient support to pass the measure through Congress in May, 1854.

Although the South received the law with little enthusiasm it engendered a storm of disapproval in the North. Often the protest was sparked by the Whigs who were happy to seize the opportunity to embarrass the long-dominant Democrats. But in many places Democrats, calling themselves Anti-Nebraska Democrats, threw off the bonds of party unity and opposed the act. Illinois, Douglas' home state, was no exception to the northern mood. Anti-Nebraska Democrats proved to be numerous in the northern and central parts of the state. Trumbull was quick to join with them since he was no friend to slavery extension. In fact, as an attorney he had played a leading part in eliminating from the state the last vestiges of slavery which had crept into Illinois during the territorial days. He came forward as the Anti-Nebraska candidate for Congress in the Alton district where he had moved in 1848. After a vigorous campaign with Whig support he triumphed easily over the regular Democratic nominee.

If the struggle against the Kansas-Nebraska Act was an elixir for Trumbull's blighted career, the fray also enabled Lincoln to re-emerge as a leading politician in Illinois. Lincoln's anti-war stand as a Whig congressman during the Mexican War had left him unpopular and "unavailable" for further preferment. Now Lincoln also emerged from his involuntary retirement and handily won a legislative seat. Lincoln had his eyes set upon more than a term as a legislator. Indeed he resigned without taking his place when he thought it might hurt his chances to receive the senatorial election when it became clear that the regular Democrats would not have control on a joint ballot of the Legislature.

But if Whig Lincoln was seeking the senatorial toga as an Anti-Nebraskaite he found opposition for the honor from the same side of that question. A small group of five Anti-Nebraska Democrats was determined that no Whig should be elected and selected a candidate of their own, Lyman Trumbull. Since they appeared to hold the balance of power between the regular Democrats and the Whigs it seemed possible that they could dictate the choice of senator. Their objection to Lincoln was not personal, but they felt that the Whig party in Illinois was not sufficiently Anti-Nebraska.

As a result three formal candidates were presented to the Legislature's ninety-nine present and voting members. They were James Shields, the incumbent regular Democrat; Abraham Lincoln, the choice of the Whigs and a small number of miscellaneous Anti-Nebraska men, elected under various labels, who had caucused with the Whigs; and Lyman Trumbull, the choice of the five splinter Anti-Nebraska Democrats.

In the balloting that followed, the Anti-Nebraska Democrats, clinging stubbornly to Trumbull, blocked the election of either Shields or Lincoln. Finally, the regular Democrats dropped Shields in favor of the then Governor, Joel A. Matteson, since it seemed Matteson might eventually win over some of Trumbull's Anti-Nebraska Democrats and gain the election. Lincoln, after much soul-searching, passed the word to the Whigs to vote for Trumbull in order that the Anti-Nebraska principle might triumph.

The Lincoln-Trumbull relationship was at a crossroads. Lincoln could have let his defeat poison his future relations with Trumbull. Indeed, many of his Whig friends were indignant, claiming that the Anti-Nebraska Democrats had "stolen" the election. Lincoln was too worldly and shrewd a politician to adopt this attitude, and at a chance meeting with Trumbull the very night of the election he warmly congratulated the victor. Moreover, Lincoln soon opened a warm and friendly correspondence with Trumbull which continued regularly until Lincoln was inaugurated President in 1861.

From his election in January, 1855, until the spring of 1856, Trumbull clung tenaciously to the label of Anti-Nebraska Democrat. He spurned the small and noisy group called "Republicans" who had organized themselves into a party in Illinois in 1854. They were considered out-and-out abolitionists and throughout the state and except in northern Illinois they were an insignificant minority. It was both in keeping with Trumbull's political theories, as well as prudent for a politician from central-southern Illinois, to keep away from them. For his own part, Lincoln kept the Republicans in Illinois at a distance and maintained his position as a Whig.

By the spring of 1856, however, both Trumbull and Lincoln were drawn inexorably into the ranks of a modified and softened Illinois Republican party. For Trumbull the choice gradually became clear. Snubbed by the Democrats as a renegade his future within the party seemed impossible. Nationally the organization calling itself Republican fell into control of moderate men who opposed the extension of slavery but who eschewed any attempt to tamper with it inside the states where it already existed. Therefore, Trumbull drifted into the Republican party. Lincoln found it difficult to accept the new Republican party as the political group in which to operate. But as the Whig party slowly dissolved, Lincoln's hand was forced. His choice lay in accepting the pro-Nebraska Democratic party or the upstart, relatively mild, anti-slavery Republican group, since he shunned any affiliation with nativist groups who served as political decompression chambers wherein the partyless Whigs could find shelter while they decided what stand to take upon slavery.

As Lincoln became entrenched in the new organization he co-operated with Trumbull to keep the National Republican Convention conservative in candidates and platform. At Lincoln's suggestion, Trumbull attended the Philadelphia nominating convention of the Republican party in 1856. Present as an observer, Trumbull was pleased by John C. Frémont's nomination for President and regarded the platform as acceptable. Apparently he had no connection with the sizeable but unsuccessful boom which suddenly developed for Lincoln for second place on the ticket.

After Congress adjourned Trumbull returned to Illinois to campaign for the new Republican party. He and Lincoln agreed to avoid joint appearances ostensibly to cover more ground, but actually to avoid fanning the latent jealousy between their supporters into an active flame. However, at both Alton and Peoria the enterprising local committees succeeded in quietly scheduling both speakers, each without the other's knowledge. Fortunately their joint appearances broke open no old wounds. In 1856 the Illinois Democrats carried the state for their successful presidential candidate James Buchanan, but only by 9,000 votes. The Republican state ticket crept to a narrow victory. This early success heartened the Republicans.

During the Buchanan administration Trumbull continued his role in Congress as a staunch Republican, excoriating President Buchanan and his works. The situation in frontier Kansas simmered on with clashes between the rival groups dedicated to making Kansas slave or free.

In the summer of 1857 Trumbull made a major address to the Illinois Republicans in the state capitol. The U. S. Supreme Court earlier that year had enunciated its Dred Scott decision, which seemed to say that no federal law could ban slavery from a territory. If this were taken at face value the Republican party had no reason for being, since its announced object was unconstitutional. In his speech Trumbull had no qualms about denouncing the opinion; throughout his career he argued that the courts were not a suitable forum to settle political questions.

Even in the East, Trumbull's speech attracted wide attention. The New York *Herald,* a Buchanan paper, admitted, "In fact, Senator Trumbull, as a statesman-like reasoner upon the great public question of the day, is no only more than a match for Mr. Douglas . . . but as a learned and practical expounder of the principles of his party he eclipses Wm. H. Seward. . . ."

Many politicians in Illinois were hardly less effusive in their praise Gustave Koerner, German-American Republican leader, a harsh realist who seldom bothered to flatter anyone, compared Trumbull's address to a speech recently made upon the same subject by Lincoln and termed Trumbull's better, saying, "Lincoln's speech is too much on the old conservative order."

Meanwhile events came to a crisis in Kansas. The pro-slavery faction succeeded in holding a constitutional convention and adopted a state constitution which protected slavery in Kansas. Then they sent the constitution to President Buchanan and clamored for immediate admission as a slave state. Buchanan decided to accept the Lecompton action asking Congress to admit Kansas as a slave state. For his part, Douglas denounced the Lecompton Constitution as a perversion of his "popular sovereignty." This brought Douglas over to roughly the Republican position. Some eastern Republicans hailed Douglas and welcomed him to stand for re-election to the Senate as a Republican. This alarmed Lincoln since it had been agreed that he should have the chance to unseat Douglas. Trumbull concurred with Lincoln that Douglas would not do as a Republican candidate. So the two worked together to discourage Republican backing for Douglas. In addition Trumbull pledged his unswerving support to Lincoln for the Senate And in the congressional hurly-burly that followed and ended in the rejection of the Lecompton Constitution, Trumbull carefully tried to define the Republican position so as to exclude Douglas.

When the congressional session of 1858 ended, the skirmishing of the Illinois senatorial campaign had already begun. Eventually the Republicans stood firmly behind Lincoln as their senatorial choice, but Douglas was not left without party support since his cohorts easily captured control of the regular organization from the supporters of President Buchanan and the so-called National Democrats. The friends of Buchanan, by then the mortal foes of Douglas, made arrangements to run candidates for the Legislature which would elect the new senator. They could not hope to win but endeavored to draw off vital votes from the Douglasites.

In the end the National Democrats proved a negligible factor and disappointment to the Republicans as their strength was approximately only that of the federal officeholders.

Trumbull stumped Illinois extensively upon Lincoln's behalf in the canvass of 1858. It is noteworthy that Trumbull's speeches, upon a close reading, stand revealed as more anti-Douglas than pro-Lincoln.

At first Trumbull's running verbal battle with Douglas captured the center of the stage, but the Lincoln-Douglas debates, as Lincoln intended, soon took the spotlight. Even there Trumbull's name cropped up frequently. Douglas was fond of charging that Lincoln and Trumbull had made a bargain in 1855. According to Douglas' story Lincoln was to get the senatorship at that time in place of Shields with Trumbull waiting until 1858-59 to try to best Douglas. But Douglas averred Trumbull then had treacherously turned on Lincoln, seizing the senatorship for himself. Categorically Lincoln denied any such arrangement each time Douglas raised the issue.

Because of the gerrymandered apportionment of seats the Douglasites had a clear majority in the Legislature on a joint ballot although Republican candidates for the Illinois Legislature polled some 125,000 votes to the Democrats' 121,000.

Lincoln had become a national figure, but Trumbull and indeed many others in Illinois were slow to recognize his new status. Lincoln appreciated Trumbull's efforts in his behalf and as evidence of his kind feeling for the Senator he wrote a letter to Norman Judd, a staunch Trumbull supporter, only days after the November election calling for a strenuous effort to end the gerrymander by which the Democrats had won control of the Legislature with less than a popular majority. Lincoln urged that Trumbull's friends hammer at this issue or Trumbull would be as unfairly beaten in two years as he had been.

One legacy from the 1858 campaign inherited by both Lincoln and Trumbull was the malevolent desire for revenge nurtured within the veteran politician "Long John" Wentworth since he had hoped to be the Republican senatorial candidate. Wentworth mapped a plan of vengeance; he would split the Republican party into its component parts, former Whigs and former Democrats. To this end he authored an article which he desired to place in some paper other than his own in order to give it authenticity. In this article he alleged that former Democrats like Trumbull were

71

trying to dominate the Republican party and cheat ex-Whigs like Lincoln out of their rightful share of the party nominations. Trumbull learning of Wentworth's plot, warned Lincoln of the mischief-making afoot. Lincoln replied promptly in a warm letter saying, "Any effort to put enmity between you and me, is as idle as the wind." He added, "I cannot conceive it possible for me to be a rival of yours, or to take sides against you in favor of any rival." When Wentworth continued his tale-bearing Lincoln declared in a letter to Norman Judd, "But I do not understand Trumbull and myself to be rivals. You know I am pledged to not enter a struggle with him for the seat in the Senate now occupied by him . . . ." This did not deter Wentworth from further intrigues but he had no major success.

As the presidential campaign of 1860 approached Trumbull was concerned that the "right" candidate be chosen. In 1860 control of the Illinois Legislature that would choose his successor would be at stake. Therefore Trumbull needed a candidate who could run swiftly, pulling the whole Republican ticket behind in the vital but mildly anti-slavery central Illinois counties. Toward the hard-running William H. Seward of New York Trumbull felt a personal aversion and, moreover, because of Seward's radical pronouncements he would be a liability in the Illinois legislative contests. Salmon P. Chase, another hopeful, would not do for the reason that he was as radical in fact as Seward seemed. Trumbull felt drawn toward the aged Supreme Court Justice John McLean as a presidential candidate, and he frankly informed Lincoln of his opinion. Lincoln was by this time an open candidate, but Trumbull could not take his candidacy seriously. However, nominally he remained a Lincoln supporter since to be anything else would split the Illinois Republicans. Indeed when Trumbull's name was broached for the highest place, Trumbull promptly silenced the talk. He realized that he would never receive the undivided support of his own state delegation and that without it his chances were infinitesimal. Moreover, any attempt to contest control of the Illinois delegation with Lincoln would shatter Trumbull's chances for his cherished re-election to the Senate.

After Lincoln was nominated by the Republican Convention, Trumbull, surprised, was yet enthusiastic that Lincoln had gained the day. He clearly believed that as a newcomer to the national scene Lincoln would listen to his counsel. Consequently, in several political meetings in the

72

East while Congress was yet in session, Trumbull spoke of Lincoln in glowing terms that strongly contrasted with his mild praise during the campaign of 1858.

During the spirited campaign in Illinois in 1860, Trumbull thoroughly stumped the state in behalf of the entire Republican ticket. He was rewarded when Lincoln not only carried Illinois over the regular Democratic candidate, Stephen Douglas, and went on to national victory, but also when the Republicans won control of the Illinois Legislature which assured his own return to the Senate.

Trumbull fondly believed that Lincoln would lean on him for advice, and in the first few weeks after Lincoln's election Trumbull's expectations seemed to be realized. Lincoln conferred with him almost daily before Trumbull left for the December session of Congress. Trumbull served as Lincoln's unofficial spokesman in a speech he delivered at the Springfield victory celebration, in which Trumbull attempted to reassure the South that Lincoln would not deny it any legitimate right or the protection of the law. The effort failed, of course; the South led by South Carolina was already on the path to secession. Trumbull was spoken of widely in the press as the "right bower" of the incoming administration. Moreover, Lincoln and Trumbull journeyed to Chicago together to confer upon Cabinet appointments in the new administration with the Vice President-elect, Hannibal Hamlin.

However, after Lincoln returned to Springfield and Trumbull went on to Washington, Trumbull found more and more that he did not have Lincoln's ear. Lincoln, understandably, had to enlarge his associations beyond Trumbull. As a result Trumbull found that despite occasional letters from Lincoln he had to rely to an increasing extent upon stories in the press or even rumors to discover the President-elect's intentions. By the time that Lincoln reached Washington for the inauguration, Trumbull felt that the new President had turned away from him, relying for advice upon the Whig wing of the Illinois Republican party.

Patronage soon became a sore point between Lincoln and Trumbull. The demands made upon Trumbull by his supporters now hungry to enjoy the fruits of victory were enormous. Trumbull hated to scurry around trying to find places for his followers in the national patronage, but it was necessary if he were to retain his pre-eminent place in the Illinois Republican party. Every disappointed officeseeker blamed Trumbull personally for his being passed over, and this had a tendency to make Trumbull feel keenly that his personal prestige had directly suffered.

Trumbull had the personal goals of seeing his friend Norman Judd appointed to a place in the Cabinet and seeing William H. Seward and Simon Cameron, whom he regarded as machine politicians, excluded from the President's council. In all three cases he was disappointed. Judd was, after much hesitation, passed over while Seward became Secretary of State and Cameron became Secretary of War. This did not mean that Trumbull could not obtain for his supporters a fair share of the patronage. Indeed, Lincoln believed Trumbull had been almost embarrassingly successful by securing a land office appointment for his brother and the Dakota territorial governorship for his brother-in-law, William Jayne. Even Judd, who had been passed over for the Cabinet, found solace in securing the first nomination to a foreign service post as Minister to Prussia. In all, several dozen of Trumbull's personal followers did eventually get places. Trumbull remained miffed since he felt others, most notably Senator Edward D. Baker of Oregon, an old personal friend of the President, had received an inordinate amount of patronage.

As new friends and advisors came to share more and more of Lincoln's confidence within a month of Lincoln's inauguration, Trumbull felt excluded from the President's circle. Indeed he had already fallen into the role he was to play during most of the Lincoln administration, not that of the trusted counselor, but rather that of the gadfly who privately and even publicly slipped burrs under the saddle of the administration.

Trumbull had favored a strong stand at Fort Sumter, and when that post had been shelled and fallen to the forces of the Confederacy, he accepted willingly the issue of war. Trumbull's program soon became one of insisting upon a total effort. As a result, although he had earlier been conservative on the subject of slavery, he now became more and more an ardent critic of permitting the institution to continue. He heaped abuse upon cautious generals who in 1861 and 1862 did not seem energetic in their movements. He associated himself in his criticism of the administration more and more with the group called "Radicals" or more properly "Unconditionals" as they demanded quick action to end the war and punish the "rebels."

To Trumbull, Lincoln as a war leader was weak and vacillating. To Trumbull, Lincoln's very flexibility, which enabled him to adjust quickly to changed conditions and popular demand, seemed weakness and drift. It must be remembered that Lincoln, who eventually became a consummate leader, in the early days of the war did exhibit unsureness, hesitancy, and just plain lack of judgment in his appointments. However, in the fiery furnace of war, Lincoln eventually developed into the flexible, wisely-opportunist leader needed to take the Union through an unprecedented civil war. To Trumbull, Lincoln never seemed to have developed. Trumbull was always conscious of the Lincoln of 1855, or at least 1861, and never appreciated Lincoln's capacity to grow. And since Trumbull regarded Lincoln as a drifter and not as a leader of public opinion he therefore felt that the President was thus susceptible to the cajolery of William H. Seward, the Secretary of State. Seward had impressed Trumbull in the secession crisis of 1860-61 as an appeaser. Therefore, while the war was on Trumbull never again trusted him. As a result, in the gloomy winter of 1862-63 Trumbull played a major part in the Cabinet crisis which largely resulted from hints dropped by Salmon P. Chase, then the Radicals' darling and the Secretary of the Treasury, that Seward was responsible for much of Lincoln's seeming indecision and less than total prosecution of the war. Trumbull led the drive to force Seward out of the Cabinet. This drive failed partly because of Lincoln's ability to turn the dangerous move aside, and partly because Chase could not bring himself to say publicly what he had been saying privately to the Radical senators. Trumbull, at the famous White House confrontation of the Cabinet including Chase and the Radical senators, demanding that Seward be dismissed, was disgusted at Chase's poor performance. Trumbull was one of the few senators who dared suggest openly to Lincoln that Seward was a detriment to the war effort. When after four hours of discussion Lincoln had blunted the force of the Senators' wrath and the committee was rather lamely filing out, Trumbull felt impelled to return for a private word with Lincoln. He bluntly told Lincoln that Chase had spoken very differently about Seward the last time they had talked. It was both a warning to Lincoln and an attempt to explain why the senators acted as they had. Clearly, Trumbull felt that he had been made to look ridiculous.

Another factor in the Lincoln-Trumbull relationship was Trumbull's keen appreciation that Lincoln liked to present an innocent, even naive air which he used as a guise disarming unwary politicians. Trumbull realized that Lincoln had the faculty to use many men as tools for his policies without them being able to detect it. Indeed it often seemed to Trumbull the keener the man the sharper the tool. It was inevitable since he was discerning enough to penetrate Lincoln's guise that he should lean over backward to show that he at least was not fooled.

Nor was this all. Trumbull after he became a member of the Senate was always acutely suspicious of any president's motives and constantly watched for and dreaded any move which he construed as executive usurpation. Lincoln's system of arbitrary arrests of disloyal persons in the North, based though it was on dire necessity, was always a sore point with Trumbull. He labored incessantly in Congress until he was able to push through the *Habeas Corpus* bill of March 3, 1863, with no help and even opposition from the administration's defenders. This measure regularized the practice of arrests of suspects. And even though much of it was more honored in the breach than in the observance, Trumbull felt it to be a legal necessity.

Also when the military authorities suppressed the Chicago *Times* for its admittedly anti-war editorial policy in June, 1863, Trumbull, who had just moved to Chicago, helped mobilize public opinion against this arbitrary military action. A petition was signed and sent to Lincoln to which Trumbull and the Chicago Republican Congressman, Isaac N. Arnold, appended a postscript, which read "We respectfully ask for the above serious and prompt consideration of the President." Many Republicans denounced Trumbull and Arnold for their action in appealing to Lincoln in behalf of a notorious "copperhead" newspaper such as the *Times* unmistakably was. Under the pressure Arnold later wrote Lincoln that his action did not necessarily constitute endorsement of the protest. Trumbull never made the slightest apology for what he had done. When the postscript signed by Arnold and Trumbull arrived Lincoln was influenced by it to take a step he felt reluctant to try, that is overriding the orders of the military in the middle of the difficult days leading up to the battle of Gettysburg. However, Lincoln did intervene and the *Times* resumed publication.

Since Trumbull's action brought him under criticism from Republican party leaders, in contrast with the campaign of 1862 when he was largely inactive, he campaigned widely in Illinois in 1863, an "off" year. In this way he hoped to rehabilitate his reputation within the party.

Trumbull's relationship with Lincoln reached its perigee in the early months of 1864. In addition to political factors, Trumbull's disappointment at many of Lincoln's actions, there was one imponderable added, the bitter estrangement between Julia Jayne Trumbull and Mary Todd Lincoln. The good friends during their days as unmarried social belles of the 1840's had grown into enemies. Their friendship had not ever been close after they both married and had their own families. There is some evidence that when Lyman Trumbull was able to shunt Lincoln aside in 1855 and snatch the prized senatorship for himself it adversely affected the relations between the two wives. Still there was no open break at that time; that remained for Lincoln's presidency. During Trumbull's campaign to get a Cabinet post for Judd it clearly developed that Mrs. Lincoln was opposed to his appointment. Abraham Lincoln did not allow his wife to influence his political decisions unduly, and Judd would probably have failed of a Cabinet place anyway, but Mary Todd Lincoln's efforts against him could not have failed to cause ill feeling between her and both Trumbulls. Social rivalry and Julia's feeling that Trumbull had not received his due once Lincoln became President led to a complete estrangement by February, 1863. Even after Lincoln's tragic death the two ladies could not be reconciled, and in 1865 Mary Todd Lincoln announced that if Julia Trumbull dared to call upon her she would not be received. It is impossible to assess the amount of damage the feud of the wives brought upon the good relations of the husbands, but some damage undoubtedly resulted.

With the breakdown of his personal and political relations with the Lincolns, Trumbull felt free to speculate upon the desirability of replacing Lincoln with another candidate in 1864. Although Kate Chase Sprague, Salmon P. Chase's politically ambitious daughter, made a valiant effort to win Trumbull as an active supporter of her father by inviting him to her socially renowned parties in the winter of 1863-64, Trumbull, who had remained cordial with Chase, could never forget that Chase had flinched during the Cabinet crisis of 1862-63. Therefore, Trumbull, although he greatly admired Chase's unblinking anti-slavery attitude, could never wholeheartedly support him for the presidency.

There is much evidence that Trumbull growled and groused that Lincoln would not do for another term, as indeed many members of Congress did, but in the end he could discover no suitable alternative. He seems to have thought of himself as "available" for a draft in place of Lincoln, but the ground swell of support for him never developed to the point where he was a serious threat to the President. Trumbull remained aloof from the abortive attempt to run John Frémont as a third party candidate, and he accepted Lincoln's renomination by the Baltimore Convention. The Democrats, as a result of Trumbull's relative silence concerning his support of Lincoln, spread the word he would defect to them, but Trumbull allowed the *Illinois State Journal* to scotch the rumors for him.

Eventually in late September Trumbull took the stump for the Union (wartime name for the Republican) party. He agreed with his old political crony, George T. Brown, who had reluctantly begun to work for the re-election of Lincoln as the sole alternative to seeing the government pass into control of the peace-minded Democrats. In his speeches, Trumbull stressed the necessity of electing Union party candidates to bring the war to a victorious conclusion, but he was noticeably mild in his praise of Lincoln, the President. Since northern military victories had made a mockery of the Democratic platform statement that the war was a failure, Lincoln carried Illinois along with all of the North, except for three states, and so was triumphantly re-elected.

Despite the lack of cooperation between Lincoln and Trumbull during Lincoln's first term, it would be wrong to assume they did not on occasion work to the same purpose. In stubbornly pursuing an independent course, Trumbull often drummed a little counterpoint to Lincoln's melody. For example, Trumbull's anti-slavery agitation effectively paved the way in Illinois for an acceptance of Lincoln's Emancipation Proclamation. Trumbull's zealous advocacy of enlisting Negroes as Union soldiers prepared the ground for this administration move.

But most important of all in the case of the Thirteenth Amendment,

Trumbull, while playing a solitary hand, had effected Lincoln's purpose. By the beginning of 1864 most Republicans had become reconciled to the necessity of passing an amendment to the Constitution to finish the task Lincoln had started with the Emancipation Proclamation. Lincoln did not exert himself to push the desired amendment through the Senate. Perhaps he wished to remain aloof from the fierce intramural Republican battles there. In any event he left it to a Republican Senate to frame an amendment. John B. Henderson of Missouri had introduced the draft of a constitutional amendment which was referred to the Senate Judiciary Committee. Trumbull as chairman of the committee rewrote the wording to resemble the prohibition against slavery to be found in the Northwest Ordinance. Charles Sumner, unsatisfied with the phrasing, pressed for a version of his own. Other Republican senators were indifferent to the proposed amendment, feeling that it was purely academic so long as the Republicans lacked the necessary two-thirds majority to pass it through the House of Representatives. Trumbull fought off Sumner and the doubters with equal zeal and was rewarded when the Senate passed the amendment by a topheavy majority. Predictably the House rejected it late that spring. The matter then hung fire until after Lincoln had been re-elected on a platform that called for the passage of the amendment. Then enough Democrats bowed to the expressed view of the people, plus Lincoln's blandishments in the form of patronage, and the amendment carried in January, 1865.

With the hope of an early military victory, Lincoln in 1865 turned seriously to the problem of reconstruction. He had already set up reconstructed governments under rather generous terms in several of the southern states overrun by the North. Congress, however, had never recognized his handiwork. In the first session of the Thirty-Eighth Congress an attempt to obtain Senate recognition for the reconstructed Arkansas state government by having its senators seated had failed. Trumbull, from his vantage point as chairman of the Judiciary Committee, had played an important part in this result, although his opposition had not assumed an angry character. Lincoln took hope from this and decided, in the second session of that Congress which met in December, 1864, after his own re-election, to see if Trumbull could be brought to co-operate in reconstruction.

Trumbull, now that Lincoln had been re-elected, had no reason for disagreement on political grounds. Perhaps because Lincoln had never indulged himself in the luxury of anger at Trumbull's earlier criticisms, the Senator felt he could be gracious and accept Lincoln's proffered hand of cooperation. Lincoln's attitude toward Trumbull is graphically illustrated by an anecdote Robert Todd Lincoln recalled when questioned about Trumbull at the time of the Senator's death. Robert remembered one occasion when Trumbull had called at the White House full of complaints at how things were done. Patiently Lincoln listened, accepted some of the criticism, but then announced he felt in part his way was best and to that extent would adhere to it. After Trumbull had left, Robert asked his father why Trumbull and he could not agree when they both had the same goal, the prompt winning of the war. The President replied quietly, "We agree perfectly but we see things from different points of view. I am in the White House looking down the Avenue, and Trumbull's in the Senate looking up."

Lincoln won Trumbull's co-operation in a series of personal interviews. convincing the Senator that the reconstructed government of Louisiana would make an excellent test case. If the Louisiana senators were seated, the state government would be recognized and a precedent created whereby all of the eleven seceded states might be restored quickly and painlessly to the Union.

Perhaps the great reconstruction imbroglio might have been avoided if Trumbull could have pushed through recognition of Louisiana. In this Trumbull failed. Charles Sumner plus a handful of Radicals were joined in their opposition by several border state senators. Acting as they were from different motives, the Radicals thought reconstruction too easy under Lincoln's plan; whereas the border state senators thought it infringed too much upon state sovereignty and they filibustered the resolution to death in a crush at the end of the short congressional session despite Trumbull's valiant efforts to pass it.

Whether Lincoln and Trumbull could have continued their collaboration is a matter of question since Lincoln's early assassination after the adjournment of Congress left no time for events to give an answer.

The many Lincoln biographies which refer to Trumbull merely as a "friend of Lincoln" leave much unsaid about their relationship. Compared to Trumbull's total disgust with some of Lincoln's successors, perhaps his condemnation of Lincoln was not severe. He always insisted that Lincoln meant well but feared that he was too unsystematic, open to persuasion by shrewd manipulators like Seward, and had a program of drift, lagging seriously behind public opinion. Perhaps Trumbull remembered too well the Lincoln he had defeated in 1855, perhaps he remembered the first fumbling months of 1861 when Lincoln was feeling his way as President; in any event he never appreciated the smooth, crafty, polished manipulator of men and events that Lincoln had grown to be.

NORMAN A. GRAEBNER

Lincoln and

The National Interest

I would save the Union. I would save it the shortest way under the Constitution. The sooner the national authority can be restored the nearer the Union will be to the Union as it was. . . . My paramount object in this struggle is to save the Union. (Letter to Horace Greeley, Aug. 22, 1862.)

To Abraham Lincoln, succeeding generations of Americans have agreed, belongs the distinction of being the most successful wartime leader in the nation's history. In large measure, Lincoln's eminence rests on the peculiar significance of the problems which plagued his generation, for at issue in his presidency was the permanence of the Republic itself. Of almost equal importance in Lincoln's perennial appeal have been those personal attributes of honesty and humility, plain talk and good humor, kindness to animals, friends, and enemies, a deep sense of justice, and a devotion to the principle of freedom. Such phenomena explain why Lincoln, rather than Washington or Jefferson, has become the symbol of American democracy and the chief hero of both the nation's history and its folklore. Yet there is something ironic in this aura of devotion which surrounds the person of Lincoln, for it dims his true greatness. Surely Lincoln's character had the earmarks of nobility, but such human qualities as he possessed existed in other Americans of his day and in countless others since his death. Only the deeper consequences of his career give his qualities of person any significance at all.

Lincoln's uniqueness lay elsewhere. If it is the function of history to enlighten the decisions of the present, then Lincoln's true contribution must lie in the wisdom that characterized his phrases and guided his actions. Except for his capacity to serve ages other than his own, he would not merit the acclaim accorded him. It is precisely because Lincoln can offer some di-

83

rection to a nation troubled by unprecedented challenges abroad that he merits the attention of a grateful people. His thoughts, embodied in over a million words of letters, speeches, and state papers, are anchored to the profoundest truths of man's existence. The tragedy of Lincoln—indeed that of the Republic—rests in the persistent refusal of the country to follow his precepts. For Lincoln's statesmanship reflected the conservative and not the liberal tradition of the modern world, and nowhere was it more consistent and intelligent than in the area of foreign and military affairs.

Lincoln as President faced the necessity of resolving for his time the great debate which had characterized the nation's outlook on the world since the establishment of the Republic. Not even the Founding Fathers had agreed on the essential function of diplomacy. Was it to serve the nation's interests or its ideals? To Jefferson, in his pro-French attacks on the Washington administration, the foreign relations of a democracy dared not ignore the obligation to serve other governments which claimed a like philosophy. To him the cause of France was the cause of liberty. His disciple, James Monroe, in addressing the French Convention in 1794, declared that "republics should approach near to each other." By defending republicanism abroad, foreign policy would assure the safety of American institutions. When the independence movement erupted in Latin America after 1815, Henry Clay, then a leading member of Congress, openly supported the new cause of liberation. During the Greek war of independence in the 1820's, such distinguished Americans as Daniel Webster and Edward Everett again urged the national leadership to develop policies that would support the cause of liberty beyond American shores.

When revolution swept across Europe in 1848, it was only natural that American idealism would again burn brightly. Even in the fifties it continued to reach out to the oppressed everywhere. Said Ralph Waldo Emerson of this country's obligation to humanity: "The office of America is to liberate, to abolish kingcraft, priestcraft, caste, monopoly, to pull down the gallows, to burn up the bloody statute book, to take in the immigrant, to open the doors of the sea and the fields of the earth. . . ." Lewis Cass, the noted Michigan Democrat, introduced a resolution into the United States Senate in January, 1852, which declared that this nation would view with deep concern the efforts of European powers to crush the movements of national independence. No longer, he said, could the American Republic remain a "political cipher." It was time to demonstrate to the world that there were "twenty-five millions of people looking across the ocean at Europe, strong in power, acquainted with their rights, and determined to enforce them."

Lincoln did not escape this liberating sentiment. When Louis Kossuth, the defiant Hungarian liberal, led his people to a declaration of independence from Austrian Hapsburg rule in April, 1849, a sympathetic meeting was held in Springfield, Illinois. Lincoln reported the resolutions which extended to the revolting Hungarians this nation's "warmest sympathy" and "most ardent prayers for their speedy triumph and final success." The revolution failed, but three years later another Springfield meeting declared that "the sympathies of this country, and the benefits of its position, should be exerted in favor of the people of every nation struggling to be free. . . ." In his eulogy to Henry Clay, delivered in the Illinois State House in 1852, Lincoln said, "Mr. Clay's predominant sentiment, from first to last, was a deep devotion to the cause of human liberty—a strong sympathy for the oppressed everywhere, and an ardent wish for their elevation."

Such idealism, however accurately it reflected national sentiment, had never characterized the actual foreign policies of the Republic. The well-established diplomatic tradition which Lincoln inherited from his predecessors had never sought to serve anything but the security and welfare of the United States. Declarations of idealistic purpose had been legion, but they had never been uttered by men when they shared some responsibility for the nation's diplomacy. President Washington and Alexander Hamilton, his Secretary of the Treasury, had set the pattern of American behavior, and both of them had specifically denied the efficacy of building foreign policy on idealism. Washington declared in his Farewell Address that "it is a maxim, founded on the universal experience of mankind that no nation is to be trusted further than it is bound by its interest; and no prudent statesman or politician will venture to depart from it." To these two Federalists American policy had but one purpose—to defend the national interest. Jefferson, as President, followed this dictum closely, and Monroe, when an occupant of the White House, chided Clay for his idealism and wrote to Andrew Jackson that he would recognize the independence movement of Latin America when the aspiring nations to the south had demonstrated their ability to eliminate Spanish control. Until they could achieve this, Monroe added, they would not merit the recognition of the United States.

Lincoln accepted without hesitation this realistic tradition of American diplomacy. This did not indicate a lack of concern for humanity beyond the nation's borders. It meant, rather, that Lincoln saw no purpose in mere declarations of moral purpose. The collapse of the independence movements in Europe illustrated the limited influence of statements of righteous intent in world affairs. For Lincoln, America's contribution to human progress would be limited largely to example. The nation would fulfill its obligation to humanity by being true to itself. At Peoria in October, 1854, he expressed his apprehension "that the one retrograde institution in America, is undermining the principle of progress, and fatally violating the noblest political system the world ever saw." Slavery was wrong not only because it was "a monstrous injustice" but also because it enabled "the enemies of free institutions, with plausibility, to taunt us as hypocrites." Lincoln was concerned with the proper functioning of American democracy, for anything less would "deprive it of its just example in the world."

Shortly after the outbreak of war in 1861, Lincoln declared to John Hay that the central theme of the struggle was the necessity of proving to the world that popular government was not an absurdity. His message to Congress in July, 1861, pointed out that the outcome of the war involved more than the fate of the United States. It embraced, he said, "the whole family of man." Urging the nation to accept the burden of reforging the Union in December, 1862, he declared in cosmic terms "We shall nobly save or meanly lose the last, best hope of earth." At Gettysburg he again placed the American experiment in its world setting. He paid tribute to the dead, but what mattered, he added, was that "government of the people, by the people, and for the people shall not perish from the earth."

To Lincoln, America's mission to preserve and expand democracy did not demand any program for imposing that system on other nations and peoples. Lincoln doubted that even proselytizing would succeed. Democ racy and freedom required such precise internal conditions for acceptance by other nations that it was never clear to him how they could become suitable commodities for export. "The ultimate question as he saw it," David M. Potter has written, "was not whether the world would follow an example set by the United States, but whether the United States could rise to the challenge of setting an example of value to the world."

II

Lincoln's determination to direct his foreign policies toward the defense of the national interest did not force him to deny his practical hopes for mankind, for both could be served by the reforging of the Union. William H. Seward, Lincoln's conservative Secretary of State, accepted this momentous, if limited, objective of the administration. He wrote shortly after he entered the Cabinet, "As a statesman in the public service, I have not hesitated to assume that the Federal government is committed to maintain, preserve, and defend the Union, peacefully if it can, forcibly if it must, to every extremity." To achieve this goal he would use his full authority, even to defying any adverse sentiment in the North. "If the people of the United States have virtue enough to save the Union," he once wrote, "I shall have their virtue. If they have not, then it shall be my reward that my virtue excelled that of my countrymen."

Never before had American diplomacy faced the challenge of national survival. It mattered, therefore, what Europe's reaction to the American conflict would be. Undoubtedly most British and French leaders favored a southern triumph, for an appealing and democratic United States had long comprised a threat to both their political security and the greatness of their nations. Seward challenged whatever interest Europe had in the destruction of the American Union by assuring its rulers that such an achievement would require an exorbitant price. With the outbreak of civil war he made it clear that any recognition of the Confederacy by a European nation would mean war. He admitted bluntly to the French minister in Washington that the United States might be defeated, but France, he added, would know that it had been in a war. To Minister Charles Francis Adams in London he penned a warning for the British government: "They have misunderstood things fearfully, in Europe. Great

Britain is in great danger of sympathizing so much with the South for the sake of peace and cotton as to drive us to make war against her, as the ally of the traitors. If that comes it will be the strife of the younger branch of the British stock, for freedom against the older, for slavery. It will be dreadful, but the end will be sure and swift."

When England recognized southern belligerency in the late spring of 1861, Seward suggested with added vehemence that Adams break off his relations with the British government if it persisted in seeing the southern agents. The warning had the desired effect; the British Foreign Minister never spoke to any southern diplomat again.

Seward reminded the governments of Europe that what occurred within the United States was purely a matter of national concern. Any outside state that recognized revolution with a view to undermining the political relationships within another, he charged, "commits a great wrong against the nation whose integrity is thus invaded. . . . To recognize the independence of a new State, and so favor, possibly determine, its admission into the family of nations, is the highest possible exercise of sovereign power, because it affects in any case the welfare of two nations, and often the peace of the world." Seward reminded Europe that any other principle "would be to resolve government everywhere into a thing of accident and caprice, and ultimately all human society into a state of perpetual war." No nation, he added, "can even suffer itself to debate with parties within or without a policy of self-preservation." Europe might prolong and aggravate the struggle by exciting the hopes of those who were warring against the Union, but it could not alter the determination of the North to resist the effort with the full power of its resources. Only the corrupted nation, whatever its internal evils, ran Seward's argument, would willingly sacrifice its integrity to the strength and influence of a foreign state.

During the critical months that followed General George B. McClellan's retirement from Richmond in the spring of 1862, Seward exerted relentless pressure on those governments of Europe that anticipated the breakup of the Union. When the French Minister transmitted his government's offer of mediation to Seward in July, the Secretary warned him that "the Emperor can commit no graver error than to mix himself in our affairs. At the rumor alone of intervention all the factions will reunite themselves against you and even in the border states you will meet resistance unanimous and desperate." When the French Minister apprised Seward of Europe's confident reaction to McClellan's defeat, the Secretary stormed back, "I have noticed it, but as for us it would be a great misfortune if the powers should wish to intervene in our affairs. There is no possible compromise . . . and at any price, we will not admit the division of the Union." When the French Minister suggested that the restoration of the Union was impossible, Seward told him, "Do not believe for a moment that either the Federal Congress, myself or any person connected with this government will in any case entertain any proposition or suggestion of arrangement or accommodation or adjustment from within or without upon the basis of a surrender of the Federal Union."

When at the height of the military crisis in August, 1862, it again appeared that Europe might intervene in American affairs, Seward wrote to Adams: "The nation has a right and it is its duty, to live. Those who favor and give aid to the insurrection, upon whatever pretext, assail the nation in an hour of danger, and therefore they cannot be held or regarded as its friends. In taking this ground, the United States claim only what they concede to all other nations. No state can be really independent in any other position."

This was a sobering admission. Seward was forced to concede for a troubled nation the validity of the charge that Europe's conservatives had hurled repeatedly at American idealists—that a government cannot exist without authority and that, to maintain that authority, it must have the right to repress revolution. Americans, in their moment of travail, might have recalled the admonition of Prince Metternich, the Austrian Chancellor, uttered forty years earlier at the pronouncement of the Monroe Doctrine: "These United States . . . have cast blame and scorn on the institutions of Europe most worthy of respect. . . . In permitting themselves these unprovoked attacks, in fostering revolutions wherever they show themselves, in regretting those which have failed, . . . they lend new strength to the apostles of sedition and reanimate the courage of every conspirator."

Now the tables had turned, and Seward was forced to apply the same conservative argumentation to those Europeans who accused the North of inhumanity in suppressing self-determination in the South. Cassius Clay, the American Minister in St. Petersburg, declared that the United States was fighting for nationality and liberty. To this the *Times* of London retorted sarcastically that it was difficult to understand how "a people fighting . . . to force their fellow citizens to remain in a confederacy which they repudiated, can be called the champions of liberty and nationalism." Seward pointed to the realities of power in the American struggle and reminded Europe that if it gave expression to its moral sentiment by supporting the cause of the seemingly oppressed in America, it would merely magnify the horror and confusion. Europe's involvement, he warned in May, 1862, would not serve the interests of humanity. "If Europe will still sympathize with the revolution," he continued,

> it must look forward to the end; an end in which the war ceases with anarchy substituted for the social system which existed when the war began. What will then have become of the interests which carried Europe to the side which was at once the wrong side and the losing one? Only a perfect withdrawal of all favor from the insurrection can now save those interests in any degree. The insurrectionary state, left hopeless of foreign intervention, will be content to stop their career of self-destruction and to avail themselves of the moderating power of the Federal government. If the nations of Europe shall refuse to see this, and the war must therefore go on to the conclusion I have indicated, the responsibility for that conclusion will not rest with the government of the United States.

Lincoln and Seward understood well that the burden of preserving the Union rested solely with the American people, but they recognized also the importance of European abstention in the eventual success of northern purpose. In his famous letter of January, 1863, to the mayor and workingmen of Manchester, England, Lincoln admitted that the decisions of foreign nations "might have a material influence in enlarging and prolonging the struggle with disloyal men in which the country is engaged." But since the United States, he continued, had pursued foreign policies in the past that were generally regarded as beneficent toward mankind, it could now rely on the forbearance of others. Perhaps good will, anchored to an interest in democracy, characterized the outlook of English workingmen toward the struggle in America, but such sentiment did not determine the action of Europe's governments. It was national interest that motivated the reactions of England and France just as it actuated the threatening tone of Seward's diplomacy. Union purpose succeeded because the interests of Europe were made to coincide with those of the United States in the continued diplomatic isolation of the Confederacy.

III

Lincoln avoided moral commitments abroad that he knew American power could not fulfill. Any idealistic goals, once announced, would merely subject the government to the psychological and political pressures that always come to bear upon leaders when a particular achievement is expected of them. Whatever the impossibility of reaching such objectives, the administration would make progress toward their accomplishment or bear the charges of failure. On this realistic judgment, Lincoln refused to become involved in the effort of Polish revolutionaries early in 1863 to throw off the tyranny of the Russian Czar. The French government, under Napoleon III, sent an appeal to the United States for support in exerting "a moral influence on the Emperor of Russia." Seward responded for the Lincoln administration. In a letter to the French government of May 11, 1863, he acknowledged the American interest in public order and humanity. But he added positively, "Notwithstanding . . . the favor with which we thus regard the suggestion of the Emperor of the French, this government finds an insurmountable difficulty in the way of any active cooperation with the governments of France, Austria, and Great Britain. . . ."

Revolutionists in every country, Seward admitted, had been attracted to American democratic idealism in their search for sympathy and active support. But the United States, he continued, had never defied the counsels of President Washington that "the American people must be content to recommend the course of human progress by the wisdom with which they should exercise the powers of self-government, for-bearing at all time, and in every way, from foreign alliances, intervention, and interference." There had been many "seductions" to involve the United States in events abroad, such as the Hungarian revolution, but each appeal had been disallowed by the American government. He added: "Our policy of non-intervention, straight, absolute, and peculiar as it may seem to other nations, has become the traditional one, which could not be abandoned without the most urgent occasion, amounting to a manifest necessity. . . ." If the United States had good wishes for the progress of humanity in Europe, the nation's policy of non-intervention was not without advantage to the interests of mankind. Matters of government were internal questions, and Seward had made clear his convictions when he warned Europe not to intervene in the American Civil War.

This realistic judgment of both national power and national interest explains also Lincoln's measured reaction to Napoleon's threatened intervention in Mexico. Lincoln, in sharp contrast to many excited editors and politicians, understood clearly that the Monroe Doctrine was a viable and defensible American commitment, not because of its idealistic appeal to liberty and self-determination, but because of its accurate reflection of New World power. He refused, therefore, to involve the United States in a moral obligation by appealing to the doctrine. Instead, Seward assured Napoleon in March, 1862, that the United States had confidence in the good faith of the European nations that they would not exploit the revolutionary anarchy in Mexico by effecting a constitutional change in the Mexican government against the will of the Mexican people. Then Seward observed with profound realism:

> The President, however, deems it his duty to express to the Allies [France, England, and Spain], in all candor and frankness, the opinion that no monarchical government which could be founded in Mexico, in the presence of foreign navies and armies in the waters, and upon the soil of Mexico, would have any prospect of security or permanence.
> Secondly, that the instability of such a monarchy there, would be enhanced if the throne should be assigned to any person not of Mexican nativity. That, under such circumstances, the new government must speedily fall, unless it could draw into its support European alliances, which, relating back to the first invasion, would in fact make it the beginning of a permanent policy of armed European monarchical intervention, injurious and practically hostile to the most general system of government on the continent of America, and this would be the beginning rather than the ending of revolution in Mexico.

This warning, the Secretary added, was based on some knowledge of the political sentiments and habits of society in America. Lincoln and Seward saw that the freedom of the western hemisphere from European control had dominated the history of the preceding century. Europe would not reverse that trend successfully while the population and resources of the Americas continued their steady development. It was doubtful also, Seward chided the Europeans, that they would ever agree on any policy favorable to a counterrevolution, for their interests were too diverse. Even when the French established Maximilian of Austria as Emperor of Mexico, Seward continued to avoid any open commitment to Mexican independence. When, at the close of the Civil War in 1865, General Ulysses S. Grant urged an immediate campaign into Mexico, Seward opposed him. The Empire, he said, was crumbling; the entire episode would terminate in six months and perhaps as little as sixty days. Lincoln refused to become involved in any war that was of no vital interest to the nation. He recognized the need of hoarding the country's energy to preserve the Union, and he refused to dissipate American resources in needless involvements abroad to defend principles which must always succeed or fail on their own. Lincoln and Seward judged the power of Mexico to defend its own interests correctly. By 1866 the harrassed Napoleon was delighted to find an excuse to extricate what remained of his army from Mexico, abandoning Maximilian to the justice of his Mexican captors.

IV

War without a well-conceived political purpose becomes a senseless slaughter. It was essential, therefore, that the northern effort to subjugate the South not be anchored to goals that were beyond the power of military victory to achieve. Lincoln, in accepting this concept of limited war, would pursue the achieveable, nothing more. Nor would he suggest that paradise could evolve from endless destruction. Whatever power was available to him he would employ to satisfy no more than his clearly-defined concept of the national interest. The Union, Lincoln believed, was the one estimable goal that northern power could achieve and one commensurate with the cost of life and property that would be destroyed. "I must save this government if possible," he wrote. "What I *cannot* do, of course I *will* not do, but it may as well be understood, once for all, that I shall not surrender this game leaving any available card unplayed." In the midst of the war's fury he wrote, "I would save the Union. I would save it the shortest way under the Constitution. The sooner the national authority can be restored, the nearer the Union will be to the Union as it was. . . . My paramount object in this struggle is to save the Union."

For many in the North, Lincoln's war aims were too limited. By 1862, Republican Radicals, stimulated by the bitter emotions of war, demanded that Lincoln secure no less than a revolution in southern society. To them it was incongruous to fight a war to victory without destroying those forces of evil which allegedly had led to the conflict—slavery and the slaveholding class. It was quite obvious that the moralism which demanded such broad, humanitarian goals had a strong political motivation. Democratic victories in the elections of 1862 reduced the Republican majority in the House from 35 to 18. By aggravating and exploiting the moral convictions of the North and placing their party solidly behind the purpose of uprooting southern society, Republican leaders could relegate the Democratic party to an emotionally disadvantageous position, and reap untold political rewards whether the great moral objectives were ever really achieved or not.

Lincoln resisted all efforts to turn the struggle into a crusade. To him the Radicals harbored goals for southern society which overreached northern power. Their purpose of revolutionizing southern political and social relationships and bringing a new deal to the Negro, Lincoln feared, would merely reduce the struggle to hopeless destruction which would end in the disillusionment of those, North and South, who took such idealistic purpose seriously. Lincoln's primary concern was for the future. He doubted that good would result from a sudden derangement in the status of southern Negroes, or that the future of the Negro in the South could be resolved by the good intentions of the North. Whatever the destruction of the South and its military power, southern whites would continue to wield social, economic, and political power over the Negro whether he were slave or free. Lincoln could bring the South back into the Union; he was never convinced that he could do more.

Lincoln's conservative view toward the moral objectives of the war did not reflect an absence of conscience. Lincoln hated slavery. "If the negro is a man," he wrote, "why then my ancient faith teaches me that 'all men are created equal,' and that there can be no moral right in connection with one man's making a slave of another . . . no man is good enough to govern another man without the other's consent." But Lincoln knew also that his personal feeling toward slavery could never serve as the sole basis of sound national policy. The challenges of slavery were too fundamental and abiding to be removed by any federal policy. "If all earthly power were given to me," he said at Peoria in October, 1854, "I should not know what to do as to the existing institution." To free the slaves and deport them to Liberia, he continued, would be sending them to immediate death. To free them and make them political and social equals would defy the will of the great mass of white citizens, both North and South. "Whether this feeling accords with justice and sound judgment," he advised, "is not the sole question, if indeed, it is any part of it. A universal feeling, whether well or ill-founded, cannot be safely disregarded. We cannot, then, make them equals."

This realism determined Lincoln's wartime policies toward the South. He recognized the great dilemma that it was the racial aspect of the slave question, not slavery itself, that tormented the nation. Had the slaves been indistinguishable by color from the rest of southern society, slavery would have vanished in some previous age. In fact, it would not have flourished on American soil at all. Universal freedom, Lincoln concluded, would come hard to the South, for as an abstraction it was subject to varying interpretations. To some it meant that each man could do as he pleased; for others, that each man could do as he pleased with other men. "The shepherd drives the wolf from the sheep's throat," wrote Lincoln pointedly, "for which the sheep thanks the shepherd as a *liberator*, while the wolf denounces him for the same act as the destroyer of liberty. . . ." The issue of race posed serious questions. Under what conditions could genuine freedom for the Negro best be achieved? Could it be imposed from without unless the social, political, and economic relationships were suitable for its continuance? Power relationships within any society, Lincoln knew, were based on strongly established traditions which were seldom upset by momentary defeat in war.

There was no way in which Lincoln could guarantee human freedom or social justice for all Americans, for such ideals were limited by human nature itself. Because moral standards differ, there was no easy method of establishing divisions between good and evil. "The true rule, in determing to embrace, or reject any thing," he wrote, "is not whether it have *any* evil in it; but whether it have more of evil, than of good. There are few things *wholly* evil, or *wholly* good. Almost every thing, especially of governmental policy, is an inseparable compound of the two; so that our best judgment of the preponderance between them is continually demanded." If Lincoln detested slavery, he would not endanger the whole structure of government to remove it.

Emancipation, then, would turn on the needs of the Republic, not on the needs of the slaves. Lincoln accepted that policy only when it appeared the necessary price for the Union. Liberation was no panacea, for it could not dispose of the South's great social problem. But if it would unite the North behind the primary goal of the Union, it would be worth the cost. "It had got to be midsummer, 1862," Lincoln recalled later. "Things had gone on from bad to worse, until I felt that we had reached the end of our rope on the plan of operations we had been pursuing; that we had about played our last card, and must change our tactics, or lose the game! I now determined upon the adoption of the emancipation policy. . . ." In emancipation, as in all his other wartime measures, Lincoln attached his purpose to the interest of the nation.

Until the end of the war Lincoln continued to place the Constitution and the Union above the issue of slavery. In April, 1864, he defended his Emancipation Proclamation in a letter to a Kentucky politician: "By general law life and limb must be protected, yet often a limb must be amputated to save a life; but a life is never wisely given to save a limb. I felt that measures, otherwise unconstitutional, might become lawful, by becoming indispensable to the preservation of the Constitution, through the preservation of the nation. Right or wrong, I assumed this ground, and now avow it. I could not feel that, to the best of my ability, I had even tried to preserve the Constitution, if, to save slavery or any minor matter, I should permit the wreck of government, country, and Constitution all together." Lincoln had become convinced that he had no choice but to surrender the Union or lay "strong hand" upon the southern Negroes. "I chose the latter," he explained. "In choosing it, I hoped for greater gain than loss; but of this, I was not entirely confident. More than a year of trial now shows no loss by it in our foreign relations, none in our home popular sentiment, none in our white military force—no loss by it anyhow or anywhere. On the contrary, it shows a gain of quite a hundred and thirty thousand soldiers, seamen, and labourers. . . . We have the men; and we could not have had them without the measure."

Europe's conservative leaders never regarded Lincoln as an emancipator; to them his policy toward the slaves was nothing but a military maneuver. Lincoln himself continued to deny that he had the authority to free the slaves except as a war measure. "I am naturally anti-slavery," he observed as late as 1864. "If slavery is not wrong, nothing is wrong. I can not remember when I did not so think, and feel. And yet I have never understood that the Presidency conferred upon me an unrestricted right to act officially upon this judgment and feeling." To make his action legal in peacetime, Lincoln asked Congress in his message of December, 1864, to pass an amendment which would comprise "a fitting, and necessary conclusion to the final success of the Union cause."

Lincoln, like all statesmen of the modern world, practiced the art of the possible. This was the essence of his greatness as wielder of the nation's military and diplomatic power. As President he accepted the need of dealing with things as they were, not as he would have wished them to be. Leadership to him consisted in teaching men to accept alternatives that were always inadequate rather than in creating expectations of perfection that might destroy the limited achievements that time and circumstance would permit. Let me not promise what they ought not, he once observed, lest they be called upon to perform what they cannot. In Lincoln's leadership there was no room for the enunciation of goals which, in their elusiveness, could only have disappointed a tortured people. "In times like the present," he declared in his message to Congress in December, 1862, "men should utter nothing for which they would not willingly be responsible through time and in eternity." Men in authority, whatever the goodness of their purpose, had the fundamental obligation to be effective.

It was precisely because Lincoln expected little of the Civil War that Americans can view that struggle as a great moment in their history. For the war made its positive contribution not in the development of military science but in the realm of politics. It created the basis for a more perfect Union. That the new nation which arose from the ashes of war did not always meet the high promise of its democratic structure was not the fault of Lincoln. It was within his power to reforge the Union, to re-establish its institutions, to rekindle its traditions. To achieve more would have required the power to alter the basic character of man. This, Lincoln knew, was the one great power denied to him just as it had been denied to all men.

CLYDE C. WALTON

An Agonizing Reappraisal:

"Has the Lincoln Theme Been Exhausted?"

"Fellow-citizens, we cannot escape history. We . . . will be remembered in spite of ourselves." (From Annual Message to Congress, December 1, 1862. *Collected Works*, vol. 5, p. 537)

In January, 1936, the late James G. Randall published his influential and challenging essay "Has the Lincoln Theme Been Exhausted?" in the *American Historical Review.* After pointing out that "Lincoln is everybody's subject," and commenting upon the growing mass of literature about Abraham Lincoln, the author reached very definite answers to the question he posed: ". . . the careful scholar need not go far to discover gaps, doubts, prevalent misconceptions, unsupported interpretations, and erroneous assumptions."

The general reader, vaguely aware of the multitude of Lincoln writings, or the historian who has specialized elsewhere, might suppose that the Lincoln theme has been sufficiently developed. If, however, one finds that in the sources there is both spade work and refining work to be done, that the main body of Lincoln manuscripts is closed to research, that no definitive edition of the works is to be had, that genuine Lincoln documents are continually coming to light while false ones receive unmerited credence, and that collateral studies bearing upon Lincoln are being steadily developed, then any conclusion as to the exhaustion of the theme would appear premature. If the investigator further discovers that there are obscure points to be searched, disputed points to be pondered, lacunae to be filled, revisionist interpretations to be applied or tested, excellent studies yet to be published, others in progress, valuable projects still to be undertaken, and finally, that an adequate, full-length biography (comparable, let us say, to Freeman's new life of Lee) is still in the future, then he realizes that, far from being exhausted, the field is rich in opportunity. It will be the burden of this paper to suggest the nature of this opportunity by reviewing some of the unfinished tasks and current problems of Lincoln scholarship as they appear to the historical specialist.

Professor Randall's searching analysis of Lincoln historiography was used by many scholars as a guide to the deficiencies in our knowledge of Lincoln. The topics and areas in the "Lincoln theme" which he marked as unexplored or inadequately mined became the subjects of careful study, and one suspects that a generation of graduate students read the essay as a guide to possible dissertation topics.

It is the purpose of this paper to examine the unexplored areas and the deficiencies in the Lincoln "theme" as Professor Randall revealed them in terms of the historical scholarship of the intervening twenty-four years, and to determine if his conclusion that the study of Lincoln still is "rich in opportunity" is valid today.

*　*　*　*　*

The first area examined by Dr. Randall was that of basic and primary source materials not yet used by scholars, specifically the Robert Todd Lincoln Collection in the Library of Congress. Incorporated into his discussion of the Robert Todd Lincoln Collection were the volumes of Nicolay and Hay, *Abraham Lincoln: Complete Works.* Although the Robert Todd Lincoln Collection was sealed until 1947, Randall summarized what was known of the collection and at the same time pointed out various errors and omissions in the Nicolay and Hay version of Lincoln's works.

The Robert Todd Lincoln Collection was opened (with overwhelming fanfare) in 1947, and has been used by many scholars since—notably by Benjamin P. Thomas, Allan Nevins and Dr. Randall.[1] In 1953 appeared a superior work of scholarship which is certainly the definitive edition of Lincoln's works.[2] There is considerable reason to believe that, with the exception of "law cases and documents appertaining thereto (such as receipts for fees, affidavits, declarations, praecipes, etc.)," and a few other specified types of material, the 6,870 items in *The Collected Works* total 99 per cent of all existing Lincoln material.[3] In almost every case, the relatively few unpublished Lincoln letters located since 1953 have been of no particular significance. Some day, perhaps it will be possible to publish the known Lincoln "legal" material, but with this exception it seems most unlikely that the 1953 *Collected Works* will ever be substantially revised or expanded. The first major job pointed out by Professor Randall has been accomplished, and with superb scholarly precision.

The Robert Todd Lincoln Collection has been open since 1947,[4] but the question raised in 1936 concerning unexplored primary sources is still germane. The David Davis Papers, recently acquired by the Illinois State Historical Library, have not yet been fully explored, nor have the S. L. M. Barlow Papers in the Huntington Library. While there is no known unexplored collection of Lincoln's own letters, collections such as the Davis and Barlow papers may offer interesting opportunities to enterprising scholars. One careful student has suggested that

> Lincoln scholarship will be advanced mainly by the further exploitation of manuscript collections and other sources whose existence is already known. What is needed in some cases is no more than a careful restudy of materials which in the past have been rather heedlessly used. What is needed in other cases is a historian's instinct that can locate fruitful items in unsuspected places or a historian's imagination that can see new patterns of meaning in evidence already familiar.[5]

The questions posed in Professor Randall's essay fall into four basic groups: (1) general questions about sources and unexploited materials; (2) general questions about the men around Lincoln; (3) general questions about the events and political situations which surrounded Lincoln; (4) specific inquiries about the sources, men and events which figure in any study of Lincoln's life and times.

Many of the questions were answered by Dr. Randall's monumental *Lincoln the President;* in the *Collected Works of Abraham Lincoln* (and through the editor's painstaking investigations which were necessary before the *Collected Works* could be published); by Carl Sandburg's *Abraham Lincoln, the War Years;* Ben Thomas' *Abraham Lincoln;* the scholarly publications of the Abraham Lincoln Association; by the just published revisions of the *Day by Day* volumes; and by the works of Allan Nevins.[6] While these volumes answer many of Dr. Randall's questions, other articles and books answer almost all of the 1936 inquiries. The bibliography at the end of this article is arranged by the subjects of the questions raised by Dr. Randall, and, although not complete, is more than representative of the work done since 1936.

* * * * *

The Lincoln bibliography compiled by Jay Monaghan (1945) comprises two volumes and lists 3,958 books and pamphlets about Lincoln published prior to 1940.[7] No one knows the exact number of Lincoln books and pamphlets published since 1939. A conservative estimate might be 1,000, although some believe that the number is nearer 2,000. The periodical articles about Lincoln are literally countless, but if they were added to this calculation what would the sum of Lincoln literature be? 15,000 items? 20,000? Whatever the total, we can all agree that the sheer mass of Lincoln literature has reached staggering proportions.

Much of this literature is, of course, trivial and insignificant, or fragmentary and unsubstantiated, or irrelevant, misleading, confusing, or clearly incorrect. But from this rather scandalous accumulation of Lincolniana, both the layman and the professional scholar can learn a great deal about Lincoln. The problem, as Dr. Randall suggested, is one of selectivity.

This great literary mountain tends to obscure rather than clarify the life and times of Abraham Lincoln. Faced with this bewildering accumulation of articles, pamphlets and books, fewer and fewer of our graduate students are willing to consider the Lincoln theme as the area in which they will write their dissertations. Mistaking quantity for quality, fearful that there are no unexploited sources and that their research is actually antiquarianism, and that "everything has been done," they seem curiously reluctant to go back to the *Collected Works* and similar primary sources, to let Lincoln speak for himself. While the Lincoln doctoral dissertation may not always be important *per se,* the systematic exploration of the literature, the painstaking checking of sources one against the other under the guidance of a seasoned scholar, are invaluable in the training of those who in turn will teach in our colleges and universities. To a considerable degree, the academic future of Abraham Lincoln must rise or fall according to the research training which is being given now to the students in our graduate schools.

All of this begs the question: faced with all that has been done, is

Abraham Lincoln worth all of the time necessary to study him today? The answer must be a qualified "yes." When one studies Lincoln, one studies the middle period of American history, a period where evolution strides hand in hand with revolution. To study Lincoln is to study the problems that molded the American mind; to study Lincoln is to study the middle-western frontier, and to study the beginnings of urbanization and the rise of the railroads, to study the break up and realignment of political parties, to study immigration and the westward movement—to study, in short, much that comprises the sweep and the drama of the American dream. It goes without saying that to study Abraham Lincoln also is to study a thoroughly admirable and unique human being. And so the study of Lincoln is not only the study of one remarkable man but is at the same time the study of a critical period of American history, the period of our national growing pains, from the frontier to our only Civil War, from cabin to White House. And there can be no doubt that to study these things will lead one to a better understanding and clearer appreciation of our history.

One basic objection, however, can be made to almost any proposed research concerning Lincoln. The major outlines have already been filled in by major, creative scholars, so that generally all that lengthy, tedious research will produce is the filling in of minute details of a picture already rather well sketched. A Lincoln research project today will likely be a rehash of known information and may result in little more than a slip into a serious academic pitfall—a departure that mocks scholarship—the substitution of antiquarianism for research.

Now an antiquary, says Webster, is (1) a very old man, (2) an official custodian of antiquities, or (3) a grotesque figure. Webster also says that an antiquary is a student of old times through their relics, as monuments, remains of ancient habitation, statues, coins, manuscripts, etc.

And here is a very real danger—the chance of making the physical objects, *the remains,* more important than that which produced them.

This is the ever increasing danger: that Lincoln scholarship may develop into sheer antiquarianism. We are often told that such research is its own reward, that pure research has always been an important, abstract tool for extending the frontier of knowledge and developing mental discipline, defiantly detached from any utilitarian purpose. The past fifteen years, however, suggest that research in the physical and natural sciences will always have utilitarian value, at least in their widest applications.

But in the humanities and some of the social sciences, pure research can continue to exist untrammeled in a world troubled by intercontinental missiles and sputniks. But while the test of "what good is it" cannot and must not be applied to such research, there should be some standard by which it can be measured so that this failure to distinguish between the details of trivia and the minor facts of significance can be avoided.

Two possible measures can be suggested. First, does the proposed research promise results which will be useful to others engaged in the step-by-step building process which advances the frontier of knowledge? Second, does the proposed research promise results commensurate with the investment made in it by the student—the investment of his creatively productive time? Let us then examine new Lincoln research in these terms: will it add to the expansion of knowledge proportionately to the time invested, or could the same time and ability produce results of larger significance in some other area of American history?

Finally, we should ask ourselves this question: just how much do we want to know? Surely the answer ought not to be "everything." We are aware that "everything" is a goal both impossible and impractical, and not only because we cannot define "everything." This matter of how deeply we ought to explore any area or man needs the attention of the historical profession. It seems obvious that somewhere there must be a limit, and even though the limit differs for each subject and for each generation, still, there is a limit. We ought to try and find out what and where it is.

* * * * *

Now what does all this have to do with Lincoln scholarship, and Dr. Randall's essay, "Has the Lincoln Theme Been Exhausted?"

We do not know the limit to which we ought to pursue Lincoln, nor do we understand how to evaluate our creative research time. We recognize that almost all of the gaps pointed out by Dr. Randall have been filled. But still, many minor points are perhaps worthy of study. It has been suggested earlier in this paper that combing known manuscript collections might be rewarding. As yet we have not been able (or willing) to apply the techniques of other disciplines to Lincoln study—statistics, economics, medicine and psychiatry, all may open interesting avenues for the historian to travel. In these respects the Lincoln theme is far from exhausted.

But perhaps most important of all is the happy fact that Lincoln has become both a symbol of democracy and the outstanding American example of true greatness. Allan Nevins recently summed up the appeal of Lincoln the democratic symbol:

> With those people who think we make too much of the Lincoln anniversaries, it is difficult for a reflective man to feel any patience. As the ancient Roman household found inspiration in annually celebrating the natal day of its most illustrious ancestor, our American household finds refreshment each year in reverting to the example of its greatest exponent of democracy. For it is as the essential Hero of Democracy that we recall Lincoln.[8]

We should be equally concerned with Lincoln as the epitome of American greatness. All of the study of the letters, the documents, the newspapers, the court records, ought to help explain this matter. The thousands of books, pamphlets and articles ought to help explain this matter. After all, we know more about Lincoln's day-by-day activity than he knew; we know more about his family and ancestors than he knew. Some of our scholars may know more about the details of his life than they know of their own.

We have erected a mountain of Lincoln information which we scan page by weary page. But still we have to try to answer the riddle: What made him the man he was? In the end, perhaps we will never find out, because all of our learning is imperfect. Was it an accident of circumstance—a happenstance—when the time was right? Or was it something deep in the heart, something in his soul, that made him the Abraham Lincoln we admire? What made this man such a towering figure? We still do not know.

And this may be the reason why the research goes on, and why the Lincoln theme will never be exhausted.

NOTES

1. Thomas, Benjamin P., *Abraham Lincoln* (New York: Alfred A. Knopf, 1952); Allan Nevins, *Emergence of Lincoln*, 2 volumes (New York: Charles Scribner's Sons, 1950); James G. Randall, *Lincoln the President*, 4 volumes (New York: Dodd, Mead, 1945-1955).

2. Basler, Roy P., editor; Marion Dolores Pratt and Lloyd A. Dunlap, assistant editors, *The Collected Works of Abraham Lincoln* (New Brunswick, N. J.: Rutgers University Press, 1953-1955).

3. It is possible, however, to disagree with this estimate: See King V. Hostick "Lincoln Letters Theme Has Not Been Exhausted," *Journal of the Illinois State Historical Society*, Vol. 52, No. 1 (Spring, 1959), pp. 52-58; Roy P. Basler "A Note on the 'Lincoln Letters Theme,'" *Journal of the Illinois State Historical Society*, Vol. 52, No. 2 (Summer, 1959), pp. 307-08.

4. Mearns, David C., *The Lincoln Papers*, 2 volumes (Garden City: Doubleday, 1948).

5. An unpublished address, "The Lincoln Theme—Unexhausted and Inexhaustible," by Richard N. Current, delivered on the occasion of the publication of *Lincoln Day by Day: A Chronology*, February 11, 1960, in the Coolidge Auditorium, the Library of Congress.

6. Carl Sandburg, *Abraham Lincoln, the War Years* (New York: Harcourt, Brace & Co., 1939); the Abraham Lincoln Association sponsored the *Collected Works*, and published a facsimile of Lincoln's annotated copy of Howells' campaign *Life of Abraham Lincoln* (1938), Ben Thomas' *Lincoln's New Salem* (1934), Paul M. Angle's *Here I Have Lived: A History of Lincoln's Springfield, 1821-1865* (1935), William E. Baringer's *Lincoln's Rise to Power* (1935), *A House Dividing* (1945), *Lincoln's Vandalia* (1949), Harry E. Pratt's *The Personal Finances of Abraham Lincoln* (1943), as well as a *Bulletin*, *Papers* and a *Quarterly*. The Association also published studies of Lincoln day by day, Harry E. Pratt editing *Lincoln 1809-1839* (1941) and *Lincoln 1840-1846* (1939), Ben Thomas editing *Lincoln 1847-1853* (1936) and Paul M. Angle editing *Lincoln 1854-1861* (1933). These volumes have been expanded substantially under the general editorship of Earl S. Miers, with William E. Baringer editing *1809-1848* and *1849-1860* and Percy Powell editing *1861-1865* (Washington: Lincoln Sesquicentennial Commission, 1960). Allan Nevins, *Ordeal of the Union* (1947), *Emergence of Lincoln* (1950), and *The War for the Union* (1959).

7. Jay Monaghan, *Lincoln Bibliography 1839-1939, Collections of the Illinois State Historical Library*, Vols. XXXI, XXXII, *Bibliographical Series*, Vols. IV, V (Springfield: Illinois State Historical Library, 1945).

8. From an unpublished address by Allan Nevins at the Annual Lincoln Dinner sponsored by the Lincoln Group of the District of Columbia in co-operation with the Lincoln Sesquicentennial Commission, Washington, D. C., February 12, 1960.

BIBLIOGRAPHY

ABOLITION AND THE ANTI-SLAVERY CRUSADE

BOOKS

Aptheker, H. *To Be Free.* New York: International Publishers, 1948.

Bagley, William C. *Soil Exhaustion and the Civil War.* Washington, D. C.: American Council on Public Affairs, 1942.

Breyfogle, William A. *Make Free: The Story of the Underground Railroad.* Philadelphia: Lippincott, 1958.

Cox, E. S. *Lincoln's Negro Policy.* Richmond: William Byrd Press, 1938.

Dillon, M. L. *Anti-Slavery Movement in Illinois, 1809-1844.* Ann Arbor: University Microfilms, 1951.

Drake, Thomas E. *Quakers and Slavery in America.* New Haven: Yale University Press, 1950.

Dumond, Dwight L. *The Anti-Slavery Origins of the Civil War.* Ann Arbor: University of Michigan Press, 1939.

————, ed. *Letters of James Gillespie Birney, 1831-57.* New York: Appleton-Century Co., 1938. 2 vols.

Foner, Philip S. *Business and Slavery . . .* Chapel Hill: University of North Carolina Press, 1941.

————. *Life and Writings of Frederick Douglass.* New York: International Publishers, 1950. 4 vols.

Gill, John. *Tide Without Turning: Elijah P. Lovejoy and Freedom of the Press.* Boston: Starr King Press, 1958.

Ketring, Ruth A. *Charles Osborn in the Anti-Slavery Movement.* Columbus: Ohio State Archaeological and Historical Society, 1937.

Kilby, Clyde S. *Minority of One.* Grand Rapids, Mich.: Wm. B. Eerdmans Publishing Co., 1959.

Korngold, Ralph. *Two Friends of Man.* Boston: Little, Brown, 1950.

Kuhns, Frederick I. *The American Home Missionary Society in Relation to the Antislavery Controversy in the Old Northwest.* Billings, Mont., 1959.

Lloyd, Arthur Y. *The Slavery Controversy, 1831-1860.* Chapel Hill: University of North Carolina Press, 1939.

Mandel, Bernard. *Labor: Free and Slave; Workingmen and the Anti-Slavery Movement in the United States.* New York: Associated Authors, 1955.

Muelder, Hermann R. *Fighters for Freedom: The History of Anti-Slavery Activities of Men and Women Associated with Knox College.* New York: Columbia University Press, 1959.

Nuermberger, Ruth A. *The Free Produce Movement: A Quaker Protest against Slavery.* Durham, N. C.: Duke University Press, 1942.

Nyrdhan, H. A. *The Atlantic and Emancipation.* London: Oxford University Press, 1937.

Savage, William S. *The Controversy over the Distribution of Abolition Literature, 1830-1860.* Washington, D. C.: Association for the Study of Negro Life and History, Inc., 1938.

Siebert, W. H. *Vermont's Anti-Slavery and Underground Railroad Record.* Columbus, Ohio: Spahr & Glenn Co., 1937.

107

Simms, Henry H. *A Decade of Sectional Controversy, 1851-1861.* Chapel Hill: University of North Carolina Press, 1942.

Stampp, Kenneth M. *And the War Came: The North and the Secession Crisis.* Baton Rouge: Louisiana State University Press, 1950.

————. *The Peculiar Institution: Slavery in the Ante-Bellum South.* New York: Knopf, 1956.

Ten Broek, Jacobus. *The Anti-Slavery Origins of the Fourteenth Amendment.* Berkeley: University of California Press, 1951.

Thomas, Benjamin P. *Theodore Weld, Crusader for Freedom.* New Brunswick, N. J.: Rutgers University Press, 1950.

Wolf, Hazel C. *On Freedom's Altar.* Madison: University of Wisconsin Press, 1952.

ARTICLES

Abrams, R. H. "Copperhead Newspapers and the Negro," *Journal of Negro History,* 20:131-52, April, 1935.

Aptheker, H. "Militant Abolitionism," *Journal of Negro History,* 26:438-84, October, 1941.

————. "Negro in the Abolitionist Movement," *Science and Society,* 5, No. 1:2-23, 1941.

Atherton, L. E. "Daniel Howell Hise, Abolitionist and Reformer," *Mississippi Valley Historical Review,* 26:342-58, December, 1939.

Bean, W. "John Letcher and the Slavery Issue in Virginia's Gubernatorial Contest of 1858-59," *Journal of Southern History,* 20:22-49, February, 1954.

Beecher, Milton F. "What Were Lincoln's Thoughts Concerning Emancipation?" *Lincoln Herald,* 54:2-8, 13, Fall, 1952.

Bloore, Stephen. "Miss Martineau Speaks Out," *New England Quarterly,* 9:403-16, September, 1936.

Boyd, W. M. "Southerners in the Anti-Slavery Movement, 1800-1830," *Phylon,* 9:153-63.

Brooks, E. "Massachusetts Anti-Slavery Society," *Journal of Negro History,* 30:311-30, July, 1945.

Buchames, Louis. "The Abolitionists and the Jews," *American Jewish Historical Society Publications,* 42:131-55, December, 1952.

Cole, Charles C., Jr. "Horace Bushnell and the Slavery Question," *New England Quarterly,* 23:19-30, March, 1950.

Craven, Avery O. "Slavery and the Civil War," *Southern Review,* 4, No. 2:243-55, 1938.

Davis, G. D. "Arkansas and the Blood of Kansas," *Journal of Southern History,* 16:431-56, November, 1950.

DeVoto, B. "Easy Chair: Slavery and Secession in Relation to the Civil War," *Harper's Magazine,* 192:123-26, February, 1940.

Dillon, M. L. "Failure of the American Abolitionists," *Journal of Southern History,* 25:159-77, May, 1959.

————. "Sources of Early Antislavery Thought in Illinois," *Journal of the Illinois State Historical Society,* 50:36-50, Spring, 1957.

Dumond, Dwight L. "The Mississippi: Valley of Decision," *Mississippi Valley Historical Review,* 36:8-24, June, 1949.

Durden, R. F. "J. D. B. DeBow: Convolutions of a Slavery Expansionist," *Journal of Southern History,* 17:441-61, November, 1951.

Eaton, C. "Censorship of the Southern Mails," *American Historical Review*, 48:266-80, January, 1943.

————. "Mob Violence in the Old South," *Mississippi Valley Historical Review*, 29:351-70, December, 1942.

Filler, L. "Parker Pillsbury: An Anti-Slavery Apostle," *New England Quarterly*, 19:315-37, September, 1946.

Fisher, Miles M. "Friends of Humanity: A Quaker's Anti-Slavery Influence," *Church History*, 10:186-202, 1935.

Fladeland, Betty L. "James G. Birney's Anti-Slavery Activities in Cincinnati, 1835-37, *Historical and Philosophical Society of Ohio Bulletin*, 9:250-65, October, 1951.

Fortenbaugh, Robert. "Representative Lutheran Periodical Press and Slavery, 1831-60," *Lutheran Church Quarterly*, 8:151-72, 1935.

Foul, N. A. "Henry David Thoreau, Abolitionist," *New England Quarterly*, 19:359-71, September, 1946.

Friedel, Frank. "Francis Lieber, Charles Sumner and Slavery," *Journal of Southern History*, 9:75-93, February, 1943.

Gara, Larry. "Propaganda Uses of the Underground Railroad, 1834-61," *Mid-America*, 34:155-71, July, 1952.

Gebo, D. R. "Uncle Tom's Cabin and Biblical Ideas of Freedom and Slavery," *Negro History Bulletin*, 19:11, October, 1955.

Gluk, W. P. "Thoreau and the *Herald of Freedom*," *New England Quarterly*, 22:193-204, June, 1949.

Govan, T. P. "Slavery and the Civil War," *Sewanee Review*, 48:533-43, October, 1940.

Graebner, Norman A. "Thomas Corwin and the Election of 1848," *Journal of Southern History*, 17:162-79, May, 1951.

Green, F. M. "Northern Missionary Activities in the South, 1846-61," *Journal of Southern History*, 21:147-72, May, 1955.

Griffin, Clifford J. "The Abolitionists and the Benevolent Societies, 1831-61," *Journal of Negro History*, 44:195-216, July, 1959.

Harlow, Ralph V. "Gerrit Smith and the Free Church Movement," *New York History*, 18:269-87, July, 1937.

Harris, A. G. "Lincoln and the Question of Slavery in the District of Columbia," *Lincoln Herald*, 53:11-18, 33, Spring, 1951; 54:12-21, Spring, 1952.

Hesseltine, W. B. "Some New Aspects of the Pro-Slavery Argument," *Journal of Negro History*, 21:1-14, 1936.

Horner, Harlan H. "Lincoln Replies to Horace Greeley," *Lincoln Herald*, 53:2-10, 27, 53:14-25, Spring, Summer, 1951.

Johannsen, R. W. "Secession Crisis and the Frontier, Washington Territory, 1860-61," *Mississippi Valley Historical Review*, 39:415-40, December, 1952.

Klement, Frank. "The Abolition Movement in Minnesota, 1854-1863," *Minnesota History*, 32:15-33, March, 1951.

Levy, Leonard. "The 'Abolition Press': Boston's First Slave Review," *New England Quarterly*, 25:85-92, March, 1952.

Lofton, W. H. "Abolition and Labor," *Journal of Negro History*, 33:249-83, July, 1948.

————. "Northern Labor and the Negro during the Civil War," *Journal of Negro History*, 34:251-62, July, 1949.

Lowell, H. "C. M. Clay and the 'True American,'" *Filson Club Historical Quarterly*, 22:30-49, January, 1948.

Ludlum, R. P. "Anti-Slavery Gag-Rule in the House of Representatives, 1837-1845," *Journal of Negro History*, 26:203-43, April, 1941.

McMahon, Edward. "Lincoln the Emancipator," *Pacific Historical Review*, 5:7-25, March, 1936.

Mandel, B. "Anti-Slavery and the Southern Workers," *Negro History Bulletin*, 17:99-105, February, 1954.

———. "Calhoun, Lincoln and Labor," *Science and Society*, 18, No. 3:235-44, 1954.

———. "Slavery and the Southern Worker," *Negro History Bulletin*, 17:57-62, December, 1953.

Martin, T. P. "Conflicting Cotton Interests at Home and Abroad, 1848-1857," *Journal of Southern History*, 7:173-94, May, 1941.

Murray, R. K. "General Sherman, the Negro and Slavery," *Negro History Bulletin*, 22:125-30, March, 1959.

Owsley, F. L. "Origins of the American Civil War" (review of *Antislavery Origins of the Civil War* by D. L. Dumond), *Southern Review*, 4:609-26, October, 1942.

Perkins, D. "A Rochester Speech Which Stirred the Nation," *Genesee County Scrapbook*, 3, No. 1:1-5, Spring, 1952.

Perkins, H. C. "Defense of Slavery in the Northern Press on the Eve of the Civil War," *Journal of Southern History*, 9:501-31, November, 1943.

Portner, Stuart. "The Abolition Movement," *Mississippi Valley Historical Review*, 24:218-20, September, 1937.

Posey, W. B. "Slavery Question in the Presbyterian Church in the Old Southwest," *Journal of Southern History*, 15:311-24, August, 1949.

Quarles, B. "Breach Between Douglas and Garrison," *Journal of Negro History*, 23:144-54, April, 1938.

———. "Letters from Negro Leaders to Gerrit Smith," *Journal of Negro History*, 27:432-53, October, 1942.

———. "Sources of Abolitionist Income," *Mississippi Valley Historical Review*, 32:63-76, June, 1945.

Rayback, J. G. "American Workingmen and the Antislavery Crusade," *Journal of Economic History*, 3:152-63, November, 1943.

Roper, L. W. "Frederick Law Olmsted and the Western Texas Free-Soil Mart," *American Historical Review*, 56:58-64, October, 1950.

Shaw, A. H. "Lincoln and the Abolitionists," *Lincoln Herald*, 56:21-27, Spring-Summer, 1954.

Shepperson, G. "Free Church and American Slavery," *Scottish Historical Review*, 30:126-43, October, 1951.

Sherwin, O. "Armory of God," *New England Quarterly*, 18:70-82, March, 1945.

Smallwood, O. T. "Historical Significance of Whittier's Anti-Slavery Poems as Reflected by Their Political and Social Background," *Journal of Negro History*, 35:150-73, April, 1950.

Staiger, C. B. "Abolitionism and the Presbyterian Schism of 1837-1838," *Mississippi Valley Historical Review*, 36:391-414, December, 1949.

Stampp, K. M. "Fate of the Southern Anti-Slavery Movement," *Journal of Negro History*, 28:23-50, January, 1943.

110

————. "Historian and Southern Negro Slavery," *American Historical Review*, 57:613-24, April, 1952.

Tuttle, C. E., Jr. "Vermont and the Slavery Question," *Vermont Historical Society Proceedings*, n.s., 6:3-11, 1938.

Ware, Ethel K. "Lydia Maria Child and Anti-Slavery," *Boston Public Library Quarterly*, 3:251-75, October, 1951.

Wesley, C. H. "Participation of Negroes in Anti-Slavery Political Parties," *Journal of Negro History*, 29:32-74, January, 1944.

Wish, H. "Aristotle, Plato and the Mason-Dixon Line," *Journal of the History of Ideas*, 10:254-66, April, 1949.

Woodward, C. V. "Irony of Southern History," *Journal of Southern History*, 19:3-19, February, 1953.

Woolfolk, G. R. "Planter Capitalism and Slavery: The Labor Thesis," *Journal of Negro History*, 41:103-16, April, 1956.

Young, J. H. "Anna Elizabeth Dickinson and the Civil War: For and Against Lincoln," *Mississippi Valley Historical Review*, 31:59-80, June, 1944.

Zirkle, C. "Soil Exhaustion, the Territorial Limitation of Slavery and the Civil War," *Isis*, 34:355-59, Part 4, 1943.

GEORGE ASHMUN

Bullard, Frederic L. "Abraham Lincoln and George Ashmun," *New England Quarterly*, 19:184-211, June, 1946.

BIBLIOGRAPHY

Angle, Paul M. *A Shelf of Lincoln Books*. New Brunswick, N. J.: Rutgers University Press, 1946.

Monaghan, Jay. *Lincoln Bibliography, 1839-1939*. Springfield: Illinois State Historical Library, 1943-45. 2 vols.

See also the section "Lincoln Literature" at the end of Thomas' *Abraham Lincoln*.

Nevins, Allan, *The Emergence of Lincoln*, Vol. II, also has a brief but excellent, evaluated bibliography.

ORVILLE H. BROWNING*

Baxter, Maurice G. *Orville Hickman Browning, Lincoln's Friend and Critic*. Bloomington: Indiana University Press, 1957.

Horner, Harlan H. "Lincoln Rebukes a Senator," *Journal of the Illinois State Historical Society*, 44:103-19, Summer, 1951.

Wilson, Rufus R. "Mr. Lincoln's First Appointment to the Supreme Court," *Lincoln Herald*, 50-51:17-25, December, 1948-February, 1949.

WILLIAM E. BARTON

Barton, Bruce. "The Most Unforgettable Character I've Met," *Reader's Digest*, 69:30-35, July, 1956.

Barton, Robert. *William E. Barton—Biographer*. Chicago: The Lakeside Press, 1946; reprinted from the *Abraham Lincoln Quarterly*, June, 1946.

---

* When only a few entries appear, articles and books are not listed separately.

SALMON P. CHASE

BOOKS

Belden, Marva R. and Thomas G. Belden. *So Fell the Angels.* Boston: Little, Brown, 1956.

Donald, David H., ed. *Inside Lincoln's Cabinet : The Civil War Diaries of Salmon P. Chase.* New York: Longmans, Green, 1954.

Phelps, Mary M. *Kate Chase, Dominant Daughter: The Life Story of a Brilliant Woman and Her Famous Father.* New York: Thomas Y. Crowell Co., 1935.

ARTICLES

Belden, Marva R. and Thomas G. Belden. "Kate Was Too Ambitious," *American Heritage*, 7:40-43, August, 1956.

Bullard, Frederic L. "Garfield and Chase—Their Ideas of Lincoln," *Lincoln Herald*, 51:2-5, December, 1949.

Nichols, Roy F. "Crazy for the White House," *Saturday Review*, 37:22, June, 1954.

Roseboom, Eugene H. "Salmon P. Chase and the Know Nothings," *Mississippi Valley Historical Review*, 25:335-50, December, 1938.

Wiley, Earl W. "Governor John Greiner and Chase's Bid for the Presidency in 1860," *Ohio Archaeological and Historical Quarterly*, 58:245-73, July, 1949.

Wilson, Charles R. "The Original Chase Organization Meeting and the Next Presidential Election," *Mississippi Valley Historical Review*, 23:61-79, June, 1936.

Zornow, William F. "Lincoln and Chase: Presidential Rivals," *Lincoln Herald*, 52:17-28, February, 1950; 52:6-12, 21, June, 1950.

———. "Lincoln, Chase and the Ohio Radicals in 1864," *Historical and Philosophical Society of Ohio Bulletin*, 9:2-32, January, 1951.

CIVIL WAR—CAUSES, ECONOMICS, HISTORIOGRAPHY

BOOKS

Craven, Avery O. *Civil War in the Making, 1815-1860.* Baton Rouge: Louisiana State University Press, 1959.

———. *The Coming of the Civil War.* New York: C. Scribner's Sons, 1942; rev. ed., 1957.

———. *The Repressible Conflict, 1830-1861.* University, La.: Louisiana State University Press, 1939.

Fish, Carl Russell. *The American Civil War, an Interpretation.* London and New York: Longmans, Green, 1937.

Gray, Wood. *The Hidden Civil War: The Story of the Copperheads.* New York: Viking Press, 1942.

Lindstrom, Ralph G. *Lincoln and Prevention of War. Which 'Blundering Generation'? Which 'Irrepressible Conflict'? An Interpretation of the Lincolnian View.* Harrogate, Tenn.: Lincoln Memorial University, 1953.

Pressly, Thomas J. *Americans Interpret Their Civil War.* Princeton, N. J.: Princeton University Press, 1954.

Rockwood, George I. *Cheever, Lincoln and the Causes of the Civil War.* Worcester, Mass.: Davis Press, privately printed, 1936.

112

ARTICLES

Barnes, J. A. "Inflation: The Civil War Years," *Current History*, 24:270-75, May, 1953.

Beale, Howard K. "What Historians Have Said about the Civil War," pp. 53-102, in Social Science Research Council. *Theory and Practice in Historical Study*. New York: Social Science Research Council, 1946.

Black, R. C., III. "Railroads of Georgia in the Confederate War Effort," *Journal of Southern History*, 13:511-34, November, 1947.

Bonner, T. N. "Civil War Historians and the Needless War Doctrine," *Journal of the History of Ideas*, 17:193-216, April, 1956.

Butler, P. R. "Some Fighters and Writers from a Civil War Bookshelf," *Quarterly Review*, 285:298-312, April, 1947.

Chamberlin, William H. "The Russian and American Civil Wars," *Russian Review*, 11:203-10, October, 1952.

Coddington, E. B. "Activities and Attitudes of a Confederate Business Man: Gazaway B. Lamar," *Journal of Southern History*, 9:3-36, February, 1943.

Craven, Avery O. "The 1840's and the Democratic Process," *Journal of Southern History*, 16:161-76, May, 1950.

———. "The Price of Union," *Journal of Southern History*, 18:3-19, February, 1952.

———. "Slavery and the Civil War," *Southern Review*, 4, No. 2:243-55, 1938.

De Voto, Bernard. "Easy Chair: Revisionist Interpretation of the Civil War," *Harper's Magazine*, 192:234-37, March, 1946.

Dorpalen, A. "The German Element and the Issues of the Civil War," *Mississippi Valley Historical Review*, 27:211-24, July, 1942.

Eaton, C. "Henry A. Wise and the Virginia Fire Eaters of 1856," *Mississippi Valley Historical Review*, 121:495-512, March, 1935.

Enmale, Richard. "Interpretations of the American Civil War," *Science and Society*, 1:127-36, 1937.

Foner, Philip S. "Labor and the Copperheads," *Science and Society*, 8, No. 3:223-42, 1944.

Friedman, M. and J. G. B. Hutchins. "Role of War in American Economic Development," *American Economic Review*, 42:612-43, May, 1952.

Gates, Paul W. "The Struggle for Land and the 'Irrepressible Conflict,'" *Political Science Quarterly*, 66:248-71, June, 1951.

Geyl, Pieter. "The American Civil War and the Problem of Inevitability," *New England Quarterly*, 24:147-68, June, 1951.

Govan, T. P. "Was the Old South Different?" *Journal of Southern History*, 21:447-55, November, 1955.

Harmon, George D. "Divine Right and the Defense of the Union, 1860-65," *South Atlantic Quarterly*, 45:43-60, January, 1946.

Hofstadter, Richard. "The Tariff Issue on the Eve of the Civil War," *American Historical Review*, 44:50-55, October, 1938.

House, A. V., and L. Marigault, eds. "Deterioration of a Georgia Rice Plantation during Four Years of Civil War," *Journal of Southern History*, 9:98-113, February, 1943.

Kelsey, E. O. "Civil War Bankers," *American Mercury*, 87:88-95, October, 1958.

Maguire, Edward J. "Northern Merchant Opinions and the Civil War," *History Bulletin*, 28:51-52, 60-63.

113

Man, A. P., Jr. "Labor Competition and the New York Draft Riots of 1863," *Journal of Negro History*, 36:375-405, October, 1951.

Nichols, Roy F. "American Democracy and the Civil War," *American Philosophical Society Proceedings*, 91, No. 2:143-49, 1947.

————. "1461-1861: The American Civil War in Perspective," *Journal of Southern History*, 16:143-60, May, 1950.

Orians, G. H. "Walter Scott, Mark Twain, and the Civil War," *South Atlantic Quarterly*, 40:342-59, October, 1941.

Owsley, Frank L. "The Fundamental Cause of the Civil War: Egocentric Sectionalism," *Journal of Southern History*, 7:3-18, February, 1941.

Parks, E. W. "Realist Avoids Reality: William Dean Howells and the Civil War Years," *South Atlantic Quarterly*, 52:93-97, January, 1953.

Parks, J. H. "Confederate Trade Center under Federal Occupation: Memphis, 1862 to 1865," *Journal of Southern History*, 7:289-314, August, 1941.

Pendleton, L. "Passions of War," *South Atlantic Quarterly*, 36:328-34, July, 1937.

Pomeroy, E. S. "French Substitutes for American Cotton, 1861-65," *Journal of Southern History*, 9:555-60, November, 1943.

Rainwater, Percy L. "Analysis of the Secession Controversy in Mississippi, 1854-61," *Mississippi Valley Historical Review*, 24:35-42, June, 1937.

————. "An Economic Interpretation of Secession: Opinions in Mississippi in the 1850's" (Ph.D. thesis, University of Chicago, 1936).

Saveth, E. N. "Human Element in History; Socio-economic Facts Are Not the Whole Story," *Commentary*, 6:180-85, August, 1948.

Schafer, Joseph. "Civil War Historiography: Carl Russell Fish," *Wisconsin Magazine of History*, 21:151-59, December, 1937.

Schlesinger, Arthur M., Jr. "The Causes of the Civil War: A Note on Historical Sentimentalism," *Partisan Review*, 16:969-81, October, 1949.

Simpson, A. F. "Political Significance of Slave Representation, 1787-1821," *Journal of Southern History*, 7:315-42, August, 1941.

Smith, G. W. "Some Northern Wartime Attitudes toward the Post Civil War South: The Economic Motivation of the Carpetbagger," *Journal of Southern History*, 10:253-74, August, 1944.

Stampp, Kenneth M. "What Caused the Civil War," in Richard W. Leopold and Arthur S. Link. *Problems in American History*. Englewood Cliffs, N. J.: Prentice-Hall, 1957.

Stern, Phillip Van Doren. "A Nation Dies, a Nation Is Reborn," *Collier's* 137:22-31, 94, April 27, 1956.

Stevens, P. "Real Cause and Purpose of the Civil War," *American Mercury*, 86:97-105, January, 1958.

Trexler, H. A. "Opposition of Planters to the Employment of Slaves as Laborers by the Confederacy," *Mississippi Valley Historical Review*, 27:211-24, September, 1940.

Turner, C. W. "Virginia Central Railroad at War, 1861-65," *Journal of Southern History*, 12:510-33, November, 1946.

Virtue, George O. "Marxian Interpretation of the Civil War," *Nebraska History*, 30:19-49, March, 1949.

Williams, T. Harry. "Changing History of Our Civil War," *Commentary*, 18:161-65, August, 1954.

Winston, R. W. "Was the American Conflict a War between States?" *Social Forces,* 13:379-82, March, 1935.

Worley, T. F. "The Arkansas Peace Society of 1861: A Study in Mountain Unionism," *Journal of Southern History,* 24:445-56, November, 1958.

Wright, G. "Economic Conditions in the Confederacy as Seen by the French Consuls," *Journal of Southern History,* 7:195-214, May, 1941.

CASSIUS M. CLAY

Robertson, James R. *A Kentuckian at the Court of the Tsars . . .* Berea College, Ky.: The Berea College Press, 1935.

Smiley, David L. "Abraham Lincoln Deals with Cassius M. Clay: Portrait of a Patient Politician," *Lincoln Herald,* 55:15-23, 29, Winter, 1953.

――――. "Cassius M. Clay and John G. Fee: A Study in Southern Anti-Slavery Thought," *Journal of Negro History,* 42:201-13, July, 1957.

――――. "Cassius M. Clay and Southern Abolition," *Kentucky Historical Society Register,* 49:331-36, October, 1951.

JACOB COLLAMER

Kelly, Mary L. *Jacob Collamer.* Woodstock, Vt.: The Woodstock Historical Society, 1944. 20 pp.

ROSCOE CONKLING

Chidsey, Donald B. *The Gentleman from New York: A Life of Roscoe Conkling.* New Haven: Yale University Press, 1935.

McLaughlin, A. C. "The Court, the Corporation, and Conkling: Construction of the 14th Amendment," *American Historical Review,* 46:45-63, October, 1940.

DAVID DAVIS

Flynn, William J. and Howard N. Morse. "David Davis, Justice U. S. Supreme Court in Retrospect: An Analysis, Appraisal, and Application of His More Significant Opinions," *Alabama Lawyer,* 13:392-95, October, 1952.

King, Willard L. "Riding the Circuit with Lincoln," *American Heritage,* 6:49, 104-9, February, 1955.

――――. "Estate of Abraham Lincoln: Historical Documents Reveal Record of Administrator," *Trust Companies,* 64:281-85, March, 1937.

A full biography of David Davis by Willard King is scheduled for publication in 1960.

"THE DIARY OF A PUBLIC MAN"

BOOKS

Anderson, Frank M. *The Mystery of "A Public Man": A Historical Detective Story.* Minneapolis: University of Minnesota Press, 1948.

The best edition is one edited by Frederic Lauriston Bullard with a foreword by Carl Sandburg, *The Diary of a Public Man* (Chicago: Abraham Lincoln Bookshop, 1945).

ARTICLES

De Voto, Bernard. "Diary of a Public Man" (review), *Harper's Magazine,* 190:500-503, May, 1945.

Holbrook, Stewart H. "My Grandfather Was an Accessory after the Fact," *American Scholar,* 20:57-60, Winter, 1951.

Latham, Henry C. "A Young Man's View of Lincoln and Douglas in 1861: Extracts from the Diary of Henry C. Latham, Springfield, Illinois," *Bulletin of the Abraham Lincoln Association,* 52:7-9, June, 1938.

Page, Evelyn. "The Diary of the Public Man," *New England Quarterly,* 22:147-72, June, 1949.

Price, B. M. "That Baffling Diary [H. Adams as author of the 'Diary of a Public Man']," *South Atlantic Quarterly,* 54:56-64, January, 1955.

Price, Benjamin M. "Who Wrote 'The Diary of a Public Man' [1860-61], a Seventy-two Year Old Mystery," *American Bar Association Journal,* 3:579-81.

Topper, R. N. "Has the Mystery of 'A Public Man' Been Solved," *Mississippi Valley Historical Review,* 40:419-40, December, 1953.

Woody, R. H. "Mystery of a Public Man: A Historical Detective Story [Samuel Ward as author of the 'Diary of a Public Man'] by F. M. Anderson," *South Atlantic Quarterly,* 48:491-92, July, 1949.

STEPHEN A. DOUGLAS

BOOKS

Capers, Gerald M. *Stephen A. Douglas, Defender of the Union.* Boston: Little, Brown, 1959.

Jaffa, Harry V. *Crisis of the House Divided: An Interpretation of the Issues in the Lincoln-Douglas Debates.* Garden City, N. Y.: Doubleday, 1959.

Petersen, William F. *Lincoln-Douglas, the Weather as Destiny.* Springfield, Ill.: Charles Thomas, 1943.

ARTICLES

Davis, G. D. "Douglas and the Chicago Mob," *American Historical Review,* 54:553-56, April, 1949.

East, Ernest E. "The 'Peoria Truce': Did Douglas Ask for Quarter?", *Journal of the Illinois State Historical Society,* 29:70-75, April, 1936.

Fehrenbacher, Don E. "Historical Significance of the Lincoln-Douglas Debates," *Wisconsin Magazine of History,* 42:193-99, Spring, 1959.

Hodder, F. H. "The Authorship of the Compromise of 1850," *Mississippi Valley Historical Review,* 22:525-36, March, 1936.

Johannsen, R. W. "Stephen A. Douglas, 'Harper's Magazine,' and Popular Sovereignty," *Mississippi Valley Historical Review,* 45:606-31, March, 1959.

Malin, James C., ed. "The Motives of Stephen A. Douglas in the Organization of Nebraska Territory," *Kansas Historical Quarterly,* 19:321-53, November, 1951.

Montgomery, H. "Georgia Precedent for the Freeport Question," *Journal of Southern History,* 10:200-07, May, 1944.

Nevins, Allan. "Stephen A. Douglas: His Weaknesses and His Greatness," *Journal of the Illinois State Historical Society,* 42:385-410, December, 1949.

Nichols, Roy F. "Kansas-Nebraska Act: A Century of Historiography," *Mississippi Valley Historical Review*, 43:187-212, September, 1956.
Venable, A. L. "Conflict between the Douglas and Yancey Forces in the Charleston Convention," *Journal of Southern History*, 8:226-41, May, 1942.
Wessen, E. J. "Debates of Lincoln and Douglas: A Bibliographical Discussion," *Bibliographical Society of America Papers*, 40:91-106, 146, 2d Quarter, 1946.

JOSHUA GIDDINGS
Ludlum, Robert P. "Joshua Giddings, Radical," *Mississippi Valley Historical Review*, 23:49-60, June, 1936.
————. "Joshua R. Giddings, Antislavery Radical, Part I, 1795-1844" (Ithaca, N. Y., 3 pp., abstract of Ph.D.).
Savage, William S. "The Origin of the Giddings Resolutions," *Ohio Archaeological and Historical Quarterly*, 47:20-39, January, 1938.

GOVERNORS, CIVIL WAR
Ambler, Charles H. *Francis H. Pierpont, Union War Governor of Virginia and Father of West Virginia.* Chapel Hill: University of North Carolina Press, 1937.
Davis, Stanton L. *Pennsylvania Politics, 1860-63.* Cleveland: The Bookstore, Western Reserve University, 1935.
Hesseltine, W. B. *Lincoln and the War Governors.* New York: Alfred A. Knopf, 1948.
———— and Hazel O. Wolf. "Lincoln and the Governors and States' Rights [1861-65]," *Social Studies*, 39:350-55, December, 1948.

HORACE GREELEY
BOOKS
Fahrney, Ralph R. *Horace Greeley and the Tribune in the Civil War.* Cedar Rapids, Ia.: Torch Press, 1936.
Hale, William H. *Horace Greeley, Voice of the People.* New York: Harper, 1950.
Horner, Harlan H. *Lincoln and Greeley.* Urbana: University of Illinois Press, 1953.
Isely, Jeter A. *Horace Greeley and the Republican Party, 1853-1861 . . .* Princeton: Princeton University Press, 1947.
Stoddard, Henry L. *Horace Greeley, Printer, Editor, Crusader.* New York: G. P. Putnam's Sons, 1946.
Trietsch, James H. *The Printer and the Prince: A Study of the Influence of Horace Greeley upon Abraham Lincoln as Candidate and President.* New York: Exposition Press, 1955.
Van Deusen, Glyndon G. *Horace Greeley: Nineteenth Century Crusader.* Philadelphia: University of Pennsylvania Press, 1953.

ARTICLES
Bonner, Thomas N. "Horace Greeley and the Secession Movement, 1860-61," *Mississippi Valley Historical Review*, 38:425-44, December, 1951.
Dunlap, Lloyd A. "President Lincoln and Editor Greeley," *Abraham Lincoln Quarterly*, 5:94-110, June, 1948.

117

Potter, D. M. "Horace Greeley and Peaceable Secession: A Re-examination of the New York *Tribune* Editorial Policy in 1860," *Journal of Southern History,* 7:145-59, May, 1941.

Smith, G. A., ed. "Noah Webster's Conservatism" [an exchange of letters with Horace Greeley], *American Speech,* 25:101-04, May, 1950.

Strauss, J. H. "Political Economy of Horace Greeley," *Southwest Social Science Quarterly,* 19:399-408, March, 1939.

Van Deusen, Glyndon G. "The Nationalism of Horace Greeley," in E. M. Earle, ed. *Nationalism and Internationalism.* New York: Columbia University Press, 1950.

DENNIS HANKS

Baber, Adin. *Nancy Hanks of "Undistinguished Families—Second Families."* Blomington, Ind.: 1959. (Mimeographed, 467 pp.)

Davis, Edwin D. "The Hanks Family in Macon County, Illinois (1838-1939)," *Transactions of the Illinois State Historical Society, 1939,* 112-52.

JOHN HAY

Dennett, Tyler, ed. *Lincoln and the Civil War in the Diaries and Letters of John Hay.* New York: Dodd, Mead & Co., 1939.

Mearns, David C. "Exquisite Collector, or the Scalping of Abraham Lincoln," *Journal of the Illinois State Historical Society,* 52:45-51, Spring, 1959.

Nicolay, Helen. "The Writing of Abraham Lincoln: A History," *Journal of the Illinois State Historical Society,* 42:259-71, September, 1949.

————. *Lincoln's Secretary: A Biography of John G. Nicolay {1832-1901}.* New York: Longmans, Green, 1949.

WILLIAM H. HERNDON

BOOKS

Donald, David. *Lincoln's Herndon.* New York: Knopf, 1948.

Hertz, Emanuel. *The Hidden Lincoln, from the Letters and Papers of William H. Herndon.* New York: Viking Press, 1938.

Herndon, William H. *Herndon's Life of Lincoln: The History and Personal Recollections of Abraham Lincoln as Originally Written by William H. Herndon and Jesse W. Weik, with Introduction and Notes by Paul M. Angle.* Cleveland and New York: The World Publishing Co., 1942.

Warren, Louis A. *Sifting the Herndon Sources.* Los Angeles: Lincoln Fellowship of Southern California, 1948.

ARTICLES

Donald, David. "Billy, You're Too Rampant," *Abraham Lincoln Quarterly,* 3:375-407, December, 1945.

————. "The True Story of 'Herndon's Lincoln,'" *New Colophon,* 1:221-34, July, 1948.

Randall, Ruth P. "With Malice toward None (except Lincoln's Wife)," *Saturday Review,* 37:11-13, February, 1954.

Saunders, Horace. "Abraham Lincoln's Partner, Billy Herndon," Lincoln Group of Chicago *Papers,* Series 2, 1945, pp. 145-58.
Warren, Louis A. "Herndon's Contribution to Lincoln Mythology," *Indiana Magazine of Hisotry,* 41:221-44, September, 1945.

NORMAN B. JUDD

Cuthbert, Norma B., ed. *Lincoln and the Baltimore Plot, 1861.* San Marino, Calif.: Huntington Library, 1949.
Dunlap, Lloyd A. "Lincoln Saves a Son," *Abraham Lincoln Quarterly,* 7:128-37, September, 1952.
Fehrenbacher, Don E. *Chicago Giant: A Biography of "Long John" Wentworth.* Madison, Wis.: American History Research Center, 1957.
————. "The Judd-Wentworth Feud," *Journal of the Illinois State Historical Society,* 45:197-211, Autumn, 1952.
McMurtry, Robert G. "Republican Campaign Problems of 1860," *Lincoln Herald,* 48:43-44, February, 1946.

WARD HILL LAMON

Hamand, Lavern M. "Ward Hill Lamon: 'Lincoln's Particular Friend' " (Ph.D. Dissertation, University of Illinois, 1949).
House, Albert V., Jr. "The Trials of a Ghost-Writer of Lincoln Biography: Chauncey F. Black's Authorship of Lamon's Lincoln," *Journal of the Illinois State Historical Society,* 31:262-96, September, 1938.
Thomas, Benjamin P. *Portrait for Posterity: Lincoln and His Biographers.* New Brunswick, N. J.: Rutgers University Press, 1947.
Tilton, Clint C. "Ward Hill Lamon in Bloomington, Illinois," Lincoln Group of Chicago *Papers,* Series 2, 1945, pp. 159-71.

GEORGE B. McCLELLAN

BOOKS

Hassler, W. W., Jr. *General George B. McClellan, Shield of the Union.* Baton Rouge: Louisiana State University Press, 1957.
Williams, Kenneth P. *Lincoln Finds a General.* New York: Macmillan Co., 1949-56. 4 vols.

ARTICLES

Greer, Allen J. "And An American," *Infantry Journal,* 43:329-35, 1936.
Mayhew, Lewis B. "George B. McClellan Reevaluated" (Thesis Abstract), Michigan *Dissertation Abstracts,* 12:737-38, 1952.
Overmeyer, P. H. "George B. McClellan and the Pacific Northwest Railroad Route Survey," *Pacific Northwest Quarterly,* 32:3-60, January, 1941.
Weisberger, Bernard A. "McClellan and the Press," *South Atlantic Quarterly,* 51:381-92, 1952.

EDWIN D. MORGAN

Gunderson, Robert G. "Lincoln and Governor Morgan: A Financial Footnote," *Abraham Lincoln Quarterly,* 6:431-37, December, 1951.
Hesseltine, W. B. *Lincoln and the War Governors.* New York: Knopf, 1948.

Rawley, James A. *Edwin D. Morgan, 1811-1883: Merchant in Politics.* New York: Columbia University Press, 1955.
———. "Lincoln and Governor Morgan," *Abraham Lincoln Quarterly,* 6:272-300, March, 1951.

JOHN M. PALMER

Palmer, Thomas. *A Conscientious Turncoat: The Story of John M. Palmer.* New Haven: Yale University Press, 1941.

WILLIAM H. SEWARD

Collier, T. M. "William H. Seward in the Campaign of 1860, with Special Reference to Michigan," *Michigan History,* 19:91-106, January, 1935.
Conrad, Earl. *The Governor and His Lady.* New York: G. P. Putnam's Sons, 1960.

JOHN SHERMAN

Crenshaw, O. "Speakership Contest of 1859-60: John Sherman's Election a Cause of Disruption?" *Mississippi Valley Historical Review,* 29:323-38, December, 1942.

EDWIN M. STANTON

BOOKS

Eisenschiml, Otto. *Why Was Lincoln Murdered?* Boston: Little, Brown, 1937.
Pratt, Fletcher. *Stanton, Lincoln's Secretary of War.* New York: Norton, 1953.
Williams, Ben A. *"Mr. Secretary."* New York: Macmillan Co., 1940.
The biography of Stanton begun by the late Benjamin P. Thomas is being completed by Harold Hyman and is promised by Knopf for early publication.

ARTICLES

Baringer, William E. "On Enemy Soil: President Lincoln's Norfolk Campaign," *Abraham Lincoln Quarterly,* 7:5-26, March, 1952.
Frank, S. J. "Conspiring to Implicate the Confederate Leaders in Lincoln's Assassination," *Mississippi Valley Historical Review,* 40:629-56, March, 1954.
Houser, Martin L. "Lincoln's Chief Lieutenant," *National Republic,* February, 1943, pp. 3-4, 21, 32.
Parker, Wyman W., ed. "Edwin M. Stanton at Kenyon," *Ohio Archaeological and Historical Quarterly,* 60:233-56, July, 1951.
Sproat, J. G. "Blueprint for Radical Reconstruction," *Journal of Southern History,* 23:25-44, February, 1957.

LEONARD SWETT

Pratt, Harry E. "A Beginner on the Old Eighth Judicial Circuit," *Journal of the Illinois State Historical Society,* 44:241-48, Autumn, 1951.

THURLOW WEED

Van Deusen, Glyndon G. "Thurlow Weed: A Character Study," *American Histori-cal Review*, 49:427-40, April, 1944.

————. *Thurlow Weed, Wizard of the Lobby*. Boston: Little, Brown, 1947.

————, ed. "Thurlow Weed's Analysis of William H. Seward's Defeat in the Republican Convention of 1860," *Mississippi Valley Historical Review*, 34:101-4, June, 1947.

GIDEON WELLES

Dunning, William A. *Truth in History and Other Essays* (N. Y.: Columbia University Press, 1937).

West, Richard S. *Gideon Welles, Lincoln's Navy Department*. Indianapolis: The Bobbs-Merrill Co., 1943.

————. "Watchful Gideon," *U. S. Naval Institute Proceedings*, 62:1091-97.

LINCOLN BIOGRAPHERS' PAPERS
BOOKS

Sandburg, Carl. *Lincoln Collector: The Story of Oliver R. Barrett's Great Private Collection*. New York: Harcourt, Brace, 1949.

Thomas, Benjamin P. *Portrait for Posterity: Lincoln and His Biographers*. New Brunswick, N. J.: Rutgers University Press, 1947.

ARTICLES

Alderson, William T. and Kenneth K. Bailey, eds. "Correspondence between Albert J. Beveridge and Jacob M. Dickerson on the Writing of Beveridge's Life of Lincoln," *Journal of Southern History*, 20:210-37, May, 1954.

Barbee, David R. "The Historical Importance [?] of the Lincoln Papers," *Records of the Columbia Historical Society*, 50:442-60.

Brooke, B. "Lincoln's Long Forgotten Boswell: J. H. Barrett," *Hobbies*, 63:108-9, February, 1959.

Donald, David. "Herndon and Mrs. Lincoln," *Books at Brown*, 12, Nos. 2-3, April, 1950.

Donnan, Elizabeth and Leo F. Stock, eds. "Senator Beveridge, J. F. James and Abraham Lincoln," *Mississippi Valley Historical Review*, 35:639-73, March, 1949.

LINCOLN: COMPARED WITH OTHER PRESIDENTS

Hofstadter, Richard. *The American Political Tradition and the Men Who Made It*. New York: Knopf, 1948.

Randall, James G. *The Liberal Statesman*. New York: Dodd, Mead, 1947.

————. "Lincoln's Peace and Wilson's," *South Atlantic Quarterly*, 43:151-74, June, 1943.

LINCOLN: INTERPRETED
BOOKS

Bryan, George S. *The Great American Myth*. New York: Carrick and Evans, 1940.

Craven, Avery O. *The Coming of the Civil War*. New York: C. Scribner's Sons, 1942; rev. ed., 1957.

Craven, Avery O. *Civil War in the Making.* Baton Rouge: Louisiana State University Press, 1959.

Current, Richard N. *The Lincoln Nobody Knows.* New York: McGraw-Hill, 1958.

Donald, David. *Lincoln Reconsidered: Essays on the Civil War Era.* New York: Knopf, 1956.

Eisenschiml, Otto. *Reviewers Reviewed: A Challenge to Historical Critics.* Ann Arbor, Mich.: William L. Clements Library, 1940.

——. *Why Was Lincoln Murdered?* Boston: Little, Brown, 1937.

McGlynn, Frank. *Sidelights on Lincoln.* Los Angeles: Wetzel Publishing Company, 1947.

Petersen, William F. *Lincoln-Douglas: The Weather as Destiny.* Springfield, Ill.: Charles Thomas, 1943.

Potter, David M. *The Lincoln Theme and American National Historiography.* Oxford: Clarendon Press, 1948.

Warren, Louis A. *Lincoln's Youth: Indiana Years, Seven to Twenty-one, 1816-1830.* New York: Appleton-Century-Crofts, Inc., 1959.

ARTICLES

Angle, Paul M. "The Changing Lincoln," in *John H. Hauberg Historical Essays,* compiled and edited by O. Fritiof Ander, Rock Island, Ill., Augustana Library Publications, No. 26, 1954.

Basler, Roy P. "As One Southerner to Another: Concerning Lincoln and the Declaration of Independence," *South Atlantic Quarterly,* 43:45-53, January, 1943.

——. "Lincoln and Literature," *Journal of the Illinois State Historical Society,* 52:33-44, Spring, 1959.

Beckner, Lucien. "Abraham Lincoln: Influences That Produced Him," *Filson Club History Quarterly,* 33:125-38, April, 1959.

Carleton, William G. "Sources of the Lincoln Legend [1809-65]," *Prairie Schooner,* 25:184-90, Summer, 1951.

Coulter, E. Merton. "What the South Has Done about Its History," *Journal of Southern History,* 2:3-28, February, 1936.

Donald, David. "The Folklore Lincoln," *Journal of the Illinois State Historical Society,* 40:377-96, December, 1947.

Kempf, Edward J. "Abraham Lincoln's Organic and Emotional Neurosis," *American Medical Association Archives of Neurology and Psychiatry,* 67:419-33, April, 1952.

Masters, E. L. "How to Debunk Abraham Lincoln," *American Mercury,* 37:241-44, February, 1936.

Naroll, Raoul S. "Lincoln and the Sherman Peace Fiasco—Another Fable?", *Journal of Southern History,* 20:459-83, November, 1954.

Stewart, Thomas D. "An Anthropologist Looks at Lincoln," *Smithsonian Report for 1952* (Washington, United States Government Printing Office, 1953), pp. 419-37.

LINCOLN: PROPAGANDA AND THE PRESS

BOOKS

Harper, Robert S. *Lincoln and the Press.* New York: McGraw-Hill, 1951.

Mitgang, Herbert, ed. *Lincoln As They Saw Him.* New York: Rinehart, 1956.

Noberka, John E. *The Sage of Lion's Den: An Appreciation of the Character and Career of Lyon G. Tyler and of His Writings on Abraham Lincoln and the War between the States.* New York: Exposition Press, 1958.

Pollard, James E. *The President and the Press.* New York: Macmillan Co., 1947.

Starr, Louis M. *Bohemian Brigade, Civil War Newsmen in Action.* New York: Knopf, 1954.

ARTICLES

Anderson, Arlow W. "Lincoln and the Union: A Study of the Editorials of 'Emigranten' and 'Faedaelardet,'" *Norwegian-American Studies and Records,* 15:85-121, 1949.

Bardolph, Richard. "Malice toward One: Lincoln in the North Carolina Press," *Lincoln Herald,* 53:34-45, Winter, 1952.

Cappon, Lester J. "The Yankee Press in Virginia, 1861-65," *William and Mary Quarterly,* 2d series, 15:81-88, January, 1935.

Cole, Edgar B. "Editorial Sentiment in Pennsylvania in the Campaign of 1860," *Pennsylvania History,* 4:219-34, October, 1937.

Craven, Avery O. "Southern Attitudes toward Abraham Lincoln," *Papers in Illinois History,* 1942, pp. 1-18.

Friedel, Frank. "The [New York] Loyal Publication Society: A Pro-Union Propaganda Agency," *Mississippi Valley Historical Review,* 26:359-76, December, 1939.

Harwell, Richard B. "Confederate Anti-Slavery Literature," *Lincoln Herald,* 53:22-27, 37, 40, Fall, 1951.

―――. "Propaganda for Secession: The 1860 Association and the Secession Convention of 1860," *Lincoln Herald,* 54:27-41, Winter, 1952.

Jones, John Paul, Jr. "Abraham Lincoln and the Newspaper Press during the Civil War," *Americana,* 35:459-72, July, 1941.

Krummel, Carl F. "Henry J. Raymond and the *New York Times* in the Secession Crisis," *New York History,* 32:377-98, October, 1951.

Laird, C. "Sufficient unto the Day Is the Propaganda Thereof," *School and Society,* 51:769-73, June, 1940.

Lively, J. K. "Propaganda Techniques of Civil War Cartoonists," *Public Opinion Quarterly,* 6:99-106, March, 1942.

Scott, Kenneth. "Candidate Lincoln in the New York Press," *New York Historical Society Quarterly,* 43:5-37, January, 1959.

―――. "Press Opposition to Lincoln in New Hampshire," *New England Quarterly,* 21:326-41, September, 1948.

Smith, George W. "Broadsides for Freedom," *New England Quarterly,* 21:291-312, September, 1948.

Steen, Ralph W. "Texas Newspapers and Lincoln," *Southwestern Historical Quarterly,* 51:199-212, January, 1948.

Wayne, J. L. "Copperhead Press of the Civil War," *Hobbies,* 48:108-09, July, 1943.

Weisberger, Bernard A. "Reporters for the Union," *South Atlantic Quarterly,* 50:38-50, January, 1951.

Zornow, William F. "The Attitude of the Western Reserve Press on the Re-election of Lincoln," *Lincoln Herald,* 50:35-39, June, 1948.

LINCOLN AND FOREIGN AFFAIRS

BOOKS

de Pineton, Charles A., Marquis de Chambers. *Impressions of Lincoln and the Civil War: A Foreigner's Account.* New York: Random House, 1952.

Luthin, Reinhard H. *Abraham Lincoln and the Tariff.* New York: Macmillan Co., 1944.

Monaghan, Jay. *Diplomat in Carpet Slippers: Abraham Lincoln Deals with Foreign Affairs.* Indianapolis: Bobbs-Merrill Co., 1945.

Pole, J. R. *Abraham Lincoln and the Working Classes of Britain.* London: Commonwealth-American Current Affairs Unit of the English Speaking Union, 1959.

Woldman, Albert A. *Lincoln and the Russians.* Cleveland: World Publishing Co., 1952.

ARTICLES

Bernstein, S. "Opposition of French Labor to American Slavery," *Science and Society,* 2:136-54, 1953.

Bullard, Frederic L. "A Friend in France in '61," *Lincoln Herald,* 51:33-37, June, 1949.

Button, F. L., comp. "A Canadian Editor Looks at Lincoln, *Hamilton Spectator and Journal of Commerce* between the Years 1859-1864" (typewritten mss.), Hamilton, Canada, 1941.

Claussen, Martin P. "Peace Factors in Anglo-American Relations, 1861-1865," *Mississippi Valley Historical Review,* 26:511-22, March, 1940.

Cohen, V. H. "Charles Sumner and the Trent Affair," *Journal of Southern History,* 22:205-19, May, 1956.

Durden, Robert F. "Lincoln's Radical Republican Envoy to the Hague and the Slavery Question," *Lincoln Herald,* 56:25-34, Winter, 1954.

Eckert, Erwin F. "Lincoln and Bismarck," *American-German Review,* 19:31, 32, 36, February, 1953.

Ellsworth, Edward W. "British Parliamentary Reaction to Lincoln's Assassination," *Lincoln Herald,* 60:47-57, June, 1958.

Ferris, N. L. "Relations of the United States with South America during the American Civil War," *Hispanic American Historical Review,* 21:51-78, February, 1941.

Garraty, John A. "Lincoln and the Diplomats," *Indiana Magazine of History,* 46:203-04, June, 1950.

Greenleaf, R. "British Labor against American Slavery," *Science and Society,* 17:42-58, 1953.

Hamer, M. B. "Luring Canadian Soldiers into Union Lines during the War between the States," *Canadian Historical Review,* 27:150-62, June, 1946.

Hecht, D. "Two Classic Russian Publicists and the United States," *American Slavic Review,* 4:1-32, August, 1945.

Jones, W. D. "British Conservatives and the American Civil War," *American Historical Review,* 58:527-43, April, 1953.

Marraro, Harvel R. "Italy and Lincoln," *Abraham Lincoln Quarterly,* 3:3-16, March, 1944.

Miller, August C. "Lincoln's Good-Will Ambassadors," *Lincoln Herald,* 50:17-27, 42, June, 1948.

Oliver, V. M. "Pre-Marxist Russian Radicals and the American Civil War," *Journal of Negro History*, 38:428-37, October, 1953.

Portuondo, Jose A. "The Uncommon Man: Lincoln as Seen by His Latin American Contemporaries," *Americas*, 11:20-24, January, 1959.

Quarles, Charles B. "Ministers without Portfolio," *Journal of Negro History*, 39:27-42, June, 1954.

Randall, James G. "Lincoln and John Bright," *Yale Review*, 34:292-304, Winter, 1945.

Sandon, Fred. "Canadian Appreciation of Abraham Lincoln," *Abraham Lincoln Quarterly*, 3:159-77, December, 1944.

Solberg, Marshall. "The International Aspects of Lincoln's Life," Lincoln Group of Chicago *Papers*, Series 2, 1945, pp. 117-24.

Whitridge, Arnold. "Lincoln through French Eyes," *Franco-American Review*, 2:71-86, Autumn, 1937.

LINCOLN AND FORT SUMTER

BOOKS

Swanberg, W. A. *First Blood: The Story of Fort Sumter.* New York: Charles Scribner's Sons, 1957.

Tilley, John S. *Lincoln Takes Command.* Chapel Hill: University of North Carolina Press, 1941.

ARTICLES

Barbee, David R. "The Line of Blood—Lincoln and the Coming of the War," *Tennessee Historical Quarterly*, 16:3-54, March, 1957.

Barbee, David R. and M. L. Bonham, Jr., eds. "Fort Sumter Again: Seward and Lincoln Pledge Conciliation of the South; Excerpt from Governor Morehead's Liverpool Address, 1862," *Mississippi Valley Historical Review*, 20:63-73, June, 1941.

Ramsdell, Charles W. "Lincoln and Fort Sumter," *Journal of Southern History*, 3:259-88, August, 1937.

Randall, James G. "When War Came in 1861," *Abraham Lincoln Quarterly*, 1:3-42, 1940.

Rutledge, Archibald. "Abraham Lincoln Fights the Battle of Fort Sumter," *South Atlantic Quarterly*, 34:368-83, October, 1935.

Stampp, Kenneth M. "Lincoln and the Strategy of Defense in the Crisis of 1861," *Journal of Southern History*, 11:297-323, August, 1945.

LINCOLN AND HIS SUPPORTERS

BOOKS

Luthin, Reinhard H. *The First Lincoln Campaign.* Cambridge, Mass.: Harvard University Press, 1944.

Packard, Roy D. *The Lincoln of the Thirtieth Congress* [1847-49]. Boston: Christopher Publishing House, 1950.

Riddle, Donald W. *Lincoln Runs for Congress.* New Brunswick, N. J.: Rutgers University Press, 1948.

Wakefield, Sherman D. *How Lincoln Became President.* New York: Wilson-Erikson, Inc., 1936.

Williams, Wayne C. *A Rail Splitter for President.* Denver: University of Denver Press, 1951.

Wilson, Rufus R., comp. *Intimate Memories of Lincoln.* Elmira, N. Y.: Primavera Press, 1945.

ARTICLES

Baker, Edward D. "Lincoln's Forgotten Friend," *Lincoln Herald,* 53:33-36, Summer, 1951.

Cardwell, Guy A., ed. "Bayard Taylor Campaigns for Lincoln," *Pennsylvania History,* 18:307-16, October, 1951.

Dickson, Edward A. "Lincoln and Baker: The Story of a Great Friendship," *Historical Society of Southern California Quarterly,* 34:229-42, September, 1952.

Fehrenbacher, Don E. "The Nomination of Lincoln in 1858," *Abraham Lincoln Quarterly,* 6:24-36, March, 1950.

Good, Burrow D. "The Three Musketeers—Illinois Version," *Illinois Quest,* June, 1940, pp. 14-17.

Harbison, Winfred A. "Indiana Republicans and the Re-election of President Lincoln," *Indiana Magazine of History,* 34:42-64, March, 1938.

―――. "Lincoln and Indiana Republicans, 1861-1862," *Indiana Magazine of History,* 33:278-303, September, 1937.

McClelland, S. W. "Two Whigs and the Whirligig: Friendship between Lincoln and Stephens," *Vital Speeches,* 9:307-11, March, 1943.

Schafer, Joseph. "Who Elected Lincoln? Not the German Population but Older Americans," *American Historical Review,* 47:51-63, October, 1941.

LINCOLN AND JOHNSON'S NOMINATION

Glonek, James F. "Lincoln, Johnson and the Baltimore Ticket," *Abraham Lincoln Quarterly,* 6:255-71, March, 1951.

Merrill, Louis T. "General Benjamin F. Butler in the Presidential Campaign of 1864," *Mississippi Valley Historical Review,* 33:537-70, March, 1947.

LINCOLN AND KENTUCKY

Brewer, W. M. "Lincoln and the Border States," *Journal of Negro History,* 34:46-72, January, 1949.

Dorris, Jonathan T. "President Lincoln's Treatment of Kentuckians," *Filson Club History Quarterly,* 28:3-20, January, 1954.

Kincaid, Robert L. "Kentucky in the Civil War," *Lincoln Herald,* 49:2, 11, 27, June, 1947.

Randall, James G. *Lincoln and the South.* Baton Rouge: Louisiana State University Press, 1946.

Townsend, William H. *Lincoln and the Bluegrass: Slavery and Civil War in Kentucky.* Lexington: University of Kentucky Press, 1955.

LINCOLN AND RELIGION

Fox, Gresham G. *Abraham Lincoln's Religion: Sources of the Great Emancipator's Religious Inspiration.* New York: Exposition Press, 1959.

Horner, Harlan H. *The Growth of Lincoln's Faith.* New York: Abingdon Press, 1939.

Jones, Edgar D. *Lincoln and the Preachers.* New York: Harper, 1948.

Monaghan, Jay. "Was Lincoln Really a Spiritualist?" *Journal of the Illinois State Historical Society,* 34:209-32, June, 1941.
Shelton, Harriet M. *Abraham Lincoln Returns.* New York: Evans Publishing Co., 1957.
Smith, Thomas V. *Abraham Lincoln and the Spiritual Life.* Boston: Beacon Press, 1951.
Wolf, William J. *The Almost Chosen People: A Study of the Religion of Abraham Lincoln.* Garden City, N. Y.: Doubleday, 1959.

LINCOLN AND SECESSION

Books

Nichols, Roy F. *The Disruption of American Democracy.* New York: Macmillan Co., 1948.
Perkins, Howard C. *Northern Editorials on Secession.* New York: Appleton-Century Co., 1942.
Potter, David M. *Lincoln and His Party in the Secession Crisis.* New Haven: Yale University Press, 1942.
Rainwater, Percy L. *Mississippi, Storm Center of Secession, 1856-1861.* Baton Rouge, La.: O. Claitor, 1938.
Stampp, Kenneth M. *And the War Came: The North and the Secession Crisis, 1860-1861.* Baton Rouge: Louisiana State University Press, 1950.
Tilley, John S. *The Coming of the Glory.* New York: Stratford House, 1949.
Weaver, Robert B. *The Struggle over Slavery.* Chicago: University of Chicago Press, 1938.

Articles

Crenshaw, O. "Christopher G. Memminger's Mission to Virginia, 1860," *Journal of Southern History,* 8:334-49, August, 1942.
Gunderson, R. G. "Washington Peace Conference of 1861: Selection of Delegates," *Journal of Southern History,* 24:347-59, August, 1958.
Klingberg, Frank W. "James Buchanan and the Crisis of the Union," *Journal of Southern History,* 9:455-74, November, 1943.
Phillips, U. B. "The Course of the South to Secession," *Georgia Historical Quarterly,* 20:276-306, December, 1936.
Prucha, F. B. "Minnesota's Attitude toward the Southern Case for Secession," *Minnesota History,* 24:307-17, December, 1943.
Queener, Verton M. "East Tennessee Sentiment and the Secession Movement, November 1860-January 1861," East Tennessee Historical Society *Publication 20* (1948), pp. 59-83.
Rainwater, Percy L. "Analysis of the Secession Controversy in Mississippi, 1854-61," *Mississippi Valley Historical Review,* 24:35-42, June, 1937.
Rutledge, Archibald. "Lincoln and the Theory of Secession," *South Atlantic Quarterly,* 41:370-83, October, 1942.
Shugg, Roger W. "A Suppressed Co-operationist Protest against Secession," *Louisiana Historical Quarterly,* 19:199-203, January, 1936.
Venable, A. L. "William L. Yancey's Transition from Unionism to State Rights," *Journal of Southern History,* 10:331-42, August, 1944.
Wooster, R. A. "Analysis of the Membership of Secession Conventions in the Lower South," *Journal of Southern History,* 24:360-68, August, 1958.

Zoes, R. J. "Minnesota Public Opinion and the Secession Controversy, December 1860-April 1861," *Mississippi Valley Historical Review*, 36:435-56, December, 1949.

LINCOLN AND THE BORDER STATES

Brewer, W. M. "Lincoln and the Border States," *Journal of Negro History*, 34:46-72, January, 1949.

Kincaid, Robert L. "Lincoln Allegiance in the Southern Appalachians," *Journal of the Illinois State Historical Society*, 52:164-79, Spring, 1959.

Sheeler, J. R. "Development of Unionism in East Tennessee, 1860-66," *Journal of Negro History*, 24:166-203, April, 1944.

LINCOLN AND THE ELECTION OF 1864

Aldrich, B. J. "Soldier Vote in '64," *Scholastic*, 45:13-14, November, 1944.

Glonek, James F. "Lincoln, Johnson, and the Baltimore Ticket," *Abraham Lincoln Quarterly*, 6:255-71, March, 1951

Harbison, Winfred A. "Zachariah Chandler's Part in the Re-election of Abraham Lincoln," *Mississippi Valley Historical Review*, 22:267-76, September, 1935.

Kaplan, Sidney. "The Miscegenation Issue in the Election of 1864," *Journal of Negro History*, 34:274-343, July, 1948.

March, David D. "The Missouri Radicals and the Re-election of Lincoln," *Mid-America*, n.s., 34:172-87, July, 1952.

Merrill, F. T. "General Benjamin F. Butler in the Presidential Campaign of 1864," *Mississippi Valley Historical Review*, 33:537-70, March, 1947.

Newman, L. "Opposition to Lincoln in the Elections of 1864," *Science and Society*, 8:305-27, 1944.

Randall, James G. "The Unpopular Mr. Lincoln," *Abraham Lincoln Quarterly*, 2:255-80, June, 1943.

Zornow, William F. "The Attitude of the Western Reserve Press on the Re-election of Lincoln," *Lincoln Herald*, 50:35-39, June, 1948.

————. "The Democratic Convention at Chicago in 1864," *Lincoln Herald*, 54:2-12, 40, Summer, 1952.

————. "The Kansas Senators and the Re-election of Lincoln," *Kansas Historical Quarterly*, 19:133-44, May, 1951.

————. "Lincoln and Chase: Presidential Rivals," *Lincoln Herald*, 52:17-28, February, 1950; 52:6-12, 21, June, 1950.

————. *Lincoln and the Party Divided*. Norman: University of Oklahoma Press, 1954.

————. "Lincoln, Chase, and the Ohio Radicals in 1864," *Bulletin of the Historical and Philosophical Society of Ohio*, 9:3-32, January, 1951.

————. "Lincoln's Influence in the Election of 1864," *Lincoln Herald*, 51:22-32, June, 1949.

————. "Lincoln Voters among the Boys in Blue," *Lincoln Herald*, 54:22-25, 39, Fall, 1952.

————. "Treason as a Campaign Issue in the Re-election of Lincoln," *Abraham Lincoln Quarterly*, 5:348-63, June, 1949.

128

Zornow, William F. "The Unwanted Mr. Lincoln," *Journal of the Illinois State Historical Society*, 45:146-63, Summer, 1952.
————. "Words and Money to Re-elect Lincoln," *Lincoln Herald*, 54:22-30, Spring, 1952.

LINCOLN AND THE EMANCIPATION PROCLAMATION

BOOKS

Eberstadt, Charles. *Lincoln's Emancipation Proclamation*. New York: Duschnes Crawford, Inc., 1950.
Wiley, Bell I. *Southern Negroes, 1861-1865*. New York: Rinehart, 1938.

ARTICLES

Beck, Warren A. "Lincoln and Negro Colonization in Central America," *Abraham Lincoln Quarterly*, 6:162-83, September, 1950.
Scheips, Paul J. "Lincoln and the Chiriqui Colonization Project," *Journal of Negro History*, 37:418-53, October, 1952.
Turner, M. P., Jr. "Emancipation in Retrospect and Prospect," *Negro History Bulletin*, 22:161-63, April, 1959.
Wesley, C. H. "Negroes of New York in the Emancipation Movement," *Journal of Negro History*, 24:65-103, January, 1939.

LINCOLN AND THE ILLINOIS LEGISLATURE

Baringer, William E. *Lincoln's Vandalia*. Springfield, Ill.: Abraham Lincoln Association, 1949.
Pratt, Harry E. *Lincoln in the Legislature*. Madison: Lincoln Fellowship of Wisconsin, Historical Bulletin No. 5, 1947.
————. "Lincoln's Salary in the Illinois Legislature," *Hobbies*, 45:10-11, October, 1940.

LINCOLN AND THE RADICALS

BOOKS

Current, Richard N. *Old Thad Stevens, a Story of Ambition*. Madison: University of Wisconsin Press, 1942.
Williams, T. Harry. *Lincoln and the Radicals*. Madison: University of Wisconsin Press, 1941.
Zornow, William F. *Lincoln and the Party Divided*. Norman: University of Oklahoma, 1954.

ARTICLES

Harbison, Winfred A. "President Lincoln and the Faribault Fire-Eater," *Minnesota History*, 20:269-86, September, 1939.
March, David D. "The Missouri Radicals and the Re-election of Lincoln," *Mid-America*, new series, 23:172-87, July, 1952.
Williams, T. Harry. "General Banks and the Radical Republicans in the Civil War," *New England Quarterly*, 12:268-80, June, 1939.
————. "Benjamin F. Wade and the Atrocity Propaganda of the Civil War," *The Ohio State Archaeological and Historical Quarterly*, 48:33-43, January, 1939.
Zornow, William F. "Lincoln, Chase, and the Ohio Radicals in 1864," *Bulletin of the Historical and Philosophical Society of Ohio*, 9:3-32, January, 1951.

LINCOLN AND THE SOUTH

BOOKS

Alexander, Lawrence A. *James Moore Wayne: Southern Unionist.* Chapel Hill: University of North Carolina Press, 1943.

Ashe, Samuel A'Court. *A Southern View of the Invasion of the Southern States and the War of 1861-65.* Raleigh, N. C., 1935 (?). 75 pp.

Crenshaw, O. *Slave States in the Presidential Election of 1860.* Baltimore: Johns Hopkins Press, 1945.

Dorris, Jonathan T. *Pardon and Amnesty under Lincoln and Johnson: The Restoration of the Confederates to Their Rights and Privileges, 1861-1898.* With an introduction by J. G. Randall. Chapel Hill: University of North Carolina Press, 1953.

Randall, James G. *Lincoln and the South.* Baton Rouge: Louisiana State University Press, 1946.

ARTICLES

Abbott, Martin. "Southern Reaction to Lincoln's Assassination," *Abraham Lincoln Quarterly,* 7:111-27, September, 1952.

Bestor, Arthur E., Jr., ed. "Letters from a Southern Opponent of Sectionalism [D. P. Bestor], September, 1860, to June, 1861," *Journal of Southern History,* 12:106-22, February, 1946.

Dorris, Jonathan T. "President Lincoln's Treatment of Confederates," *Filson Club History Quarterly,* 33:139-60, April, 1959.

Hobeika, John E. "The Fratricidal Strife—Through New England Eyes," *Tyler's Quarterly Historical and Genealogical Magazine,* 17:16-22, July, 1935.

Kincaid, Robert L. "Lincoln and the Loyal South . . . ," *Vital Speeches* 15:269-73, February 15, 1949.

Nye, R. B. "Slave Power Conspiracy: 1830-1860," *Science and Society,* 10, No. 3:262-74, 1946.

Wiley, Bell I. "Southern Reaction to Federal Invasion," *Journal of Southern History,* 16:491-510, November, 1950.

LINCOLN AND THE WEST

McGee, L. A. "Colorado Pioneers in the Civil War," *Southwestern Social Science Quarterly,* 25:31-42, June, 1944.

Pomeroy, E. S. "Lincoln, the Thirteenth Amendment and the Admission of Nevada," *Pacific Historical Review,* 12:362-68, December, 1943.

Tegeder, Vincent G. "Lincoln and the Territorial Patronage: The Ascendancy of the Radicals in the West," *Mississippi Valley Historical Review,* 35:77-90, June, 1948.

LINCOLN AS A LAWYER

BOOKS

Barton, Robert. *Lincoln and the McCormick Reaper Case.* Foxboro, Mass.: Foxboro Company, 1952.

Duff, John J. *A Lincoln, Prairie Lawyer.* New York: Rinehart & Co., Inc., 1960.

Kyle, Otto R. *Abraham Lincoln in Decatur.* New York: Vantage Press, 1957.

Miers, Earl S., ed., William E. Baringer and Percy Powell, asst. eds. *Lincoln Day by Day.* Washington: Lincoln Sesquicentennial Commission, 1960. 3 vols.

Smith, Elmer A. *Abraham Lincoln, an Illinois Central Lawyer: A Paper Read by Elmer A. Smith . . . at a Meeting of the Western Conference of Railway Counsel, February 13, 1945.* Chicago, 1945. 23 pp.

Whitney, Henry C. *Life on the Circuit with Lincoln.* With introduction and notes by Paul M. Angle. Caldwell, Idaho: Caxton Printers, 1940.

Woldman, Albert A. *Lawyer Lincoln.* Boston: Houghton, Mifflin Co., 1936.

ARTICLES

Bullard, Frederic L. "Lincoln and the Courts of the District of Columbia," *American Bar Association Journal,* February, 1938, pp. 117-20.

Duff, John J. "This Was a Lawyer," *Journal of the Illinois State Historical Society,* 52:146-63, Spring, 1959.

Evans, Evan A. "An Advocate for a Nation," *Wisconsin Law Review,* July, 1949, pp. 727-37.

Friend, Henry C. "Abraham Lincoln and the *National Intelligencer:* The Lawyer's Dilemma," *Commercial Law Journal,* 64:42-45, February, 1959.

―――. "Abraham Lincoln as a Receiving Attorney, Kelly vs Blackledge," *Commercial Law Journal,* 51:27-30, February, 1949.

Goldsmith, Harry. "Abraham Lincoln: Invention and Patents," *Journal of the Patent Office Society,* 20:5-33, January, 1938.

Hertz, Emanuel. "Abraham Lincoln—The Jurist of the Civil War," *New York University Law Quarterly Review,* 14:473-501, May, 1937.

Lamoreaux, Jeanne. "The Case That Made a President," *Harvester World,* February, 1953, pp. 2-4.

Parkinson, Robert H. "The Patent Case That Lifted Lincoln into a Presidential Candidate," *Abraham Lincoln Quarterly,* 4:105-22, September, 1946.

Pratt, Harry E. "Abraham Lincoln's First Murder Trial," *Journal of the Illinois State Historical Society,* 37:242-49, September, 1944.

―――. "Lincoln and Bankruptcy Law," *Illinois Bar Journal,* 31:201-16, January, 1943.

―――. "Lincoln and Douglas as Counsel on the Same Side," *American Bar Association Journal,* March, 1940, p. 214 ff.

Schaefer, Carl W. "Lincoln the Lawyer," *Lincoln Herald,* 51:2-17, June, 1949.

Sprecher, Robert A. "Lincoln as a Bar Examiner," *Illinois Bar Journal,* 42:918-22, August, 1954.

Street, A. L. H. "Abraham Lincoln's Municipal Law Cases," *American City,* 56-71, February, 1941.

Swisher, Jacob A. "Lincoln in Iowa," *Iowa Journal of History and Politics,* 43:69-84, January, 1945.

LINCOLN AS THE MILITARY LEADER

BOOKS

Bruce, Robert V. *Lincoln and the Tools of War.* Indianapolis: Bobbs-Merrill Co., 1956.

Catton, Bruce. *Mr. Lincoln's Army.* Garden City, N. Y.: Doubleday, 1951.

Houser, Martin L. *Lincoln and McClellan.* East Peoria, Ill.: Courier Printing Co., 1946. 28 pp.

West, Richard S. *Gideon Welles: Lincoln's Navy Department.* Indianapolis: Bobbs-Merrill Co., 1943.

————. *Mr. Lincoln's Navy.* New York: Longmans, Green, 1957.

Williams, T. Harry. *Lincoln and His Generals.* New York: Knopf, 1952.

ARTICLES

Ambrose, Stephen E. "Lincoln and Halleck: A Study in Personal Relations," *Journal of the Illinois State Historical Society,* 52:208-24, Spring, 1959.

Armstrong, W. P. "Lincoln as Commander in Chief," *Saturday Review of Literature,* 28:5-6, February 10, 1945.

Catton, Bruce, "Lincoln's Mastery in the Use of Volunteer Soldiers and Political Generals," *Lincoln Herald,* 57:3-11, Fall, 1955.

Freeman, Douglas S. "Who's in Command?" [Relation of the President to Military Operations] *The Atlantic,* 165:744-51, June, 1940.

Russell, Don, "Lincoln Raises an Army," *Lincoln Herald,* 50:2-15, June, 1948.

Soule, George. "How Lincoln Modernized the Science of War," *Popular Science,* 170:130-33, February, 1957.

LINCOLN AS PRESIDENT

BOOKS

Bruce, Robert V. *Lincoln and the Tools of War.* Indianapolis: Bobbs-Merrill Co., 1956.

Buckeridge, J. O. *Lincoln's Choice.* Harrisburg, Pa.: Stockpole Co., 1956.

Carman, Harry J and Reinhard H. Luthin. *Lincoln and the Patronage.* New York: Columbia University Press, 1943.

Dorris, Jonathan T. *Pardon and Amnesty under Lincoln and Johnson.* Chapel Hill: University of North Carolina Press, 1953.

Gray, Wood. *The Hidden Civil War.* New York: Viking Press, 1942.

Hyman, Harold M. *Era of the Oath: Northern Loyalty Tests during the Civil War and Reconstruction.* Philadelphia: University of Pennsylvania Press, 1954.

Milton, George F. *Abraham Lincoln and the Fifth Column.* New York: Vanguard Press, 1942.

————. *The Use of Presidential Power, 1789-1943.* Boston: Little, Brown, 1944. Pp. 107-36.

Randall, James G. *Constitutional Problems under Lincoln.* Rev. ed., Urbana: University of Illinois Press, 1951.

————. *Mr. Lincoln.* Edited by Richard N. Current. New York: Dodd, Mead, 1957.

Randall, Ruth P. *Courtship of Mr. Lincoln.* Boston: Little, Brown, 1957.

————. *Lincoln's Sons.* Boston: Little, Brown, 1955.

————. *Mary Lincoln: Biography of a Marriage.* Boston: Little, Brown, 1953.

Silver, David M. *Lincoln's Supreme Court.* Urbana: University of Illinois Press, 1956.

Wiel, Samuel C. *Lincoln's Crisis in the Far West.* San Francisco: privately printed, 1949. 130 pp.

ARTICLES

Bullard, Frederic L. "When Lincoln 'Ruled' Alone," *Proceedings of the Massachusetts Historical Society,* October, 1944-May, 1947, 68:301-49.

Catton, Bruce. "Lincoln's Difficult Decisions," *Civil War History,* 2:5-12, June, 1956.

LINCOLN AS PRESIDENT-ELECT

BOOKS

Baringer, William E. *A House Dividing.* Springfield, Ill.: Abraham Lincoln Association, 1945.

Cuthbert, Norma B. *Lincoln and the Baltimore Plot, 1861.* San Marino, Calif.: Huntington Library, 1949.

Villard, Henry. *Lincoln on the Eve of '61: A Journalist's Story by Henry Villard.* Edited by Harold G. and Oswald Garrison Villard. New York: Knopf, 1941.

Williams, Wayne C. *A Rail Splitter for President.* Denver: University of Denver Press, 1951.

ARTICLES

McCorison, Joseph L. "Impressions of the President-Elect, 1860 . . . ," *Abraham Lincoln Quarterly,* 3:291-301, June, 1945.

Roske, Ralph S. "Lincoln's Peace Puff," *Abraham Lincoln Quarterly,* 6:239-45, December, 1950.

Villard, Henry. "Lincoln at Bay," *The Saturday Evening Post,* Feb. 10, 1940, pp. 27, 47-48, 50.

LINCOLN AS PRESIDENTIAL CANDIDATE

BOOKS

Baringer, William E. *Lincoln's Rise to Power.* Boston: Little, Brown, 1937.

Kyle, Otto R. *Lincoln in Decatur.* New York: Vantage Press, 1957.

Luthin, Reinhard H. *The First Lincoln Campaign.* Cambridge, Mass.: Harvard University Press, 1944.

ARTICLES

Bullard, Frederic L. "About Lincoln's Election in 1860," *Lincoln Herald,* 48:5-6, December, 1946.

————. "Lincoln's 'Conquest' of New England," *Abraham Lincoln Quarterly,* 2:49-79, June, 1942.

James, Harold P. "Election Time in Illinois, 1860," *Lincoln Herald,* 49:12-21, 32, June, 1947.

————. "Lincoln and Douglas in Their Home State," *Lincoln Herald,* 49:2-9, October, 1947; 49:12-20, 26, December, 1947.

————. "Lincoln's Own State in the Election of 1860" (abstract of thesis). Urbana, Ill., 1943.

————. "Political Pageantry in the Campaign of 1860 in Illinois," *Abraham Lincoln Quarterly,* 4:313-47, September, 1947.

Johnson, H. B. "Election of 1860 and the Germans in Minnesota," *Minnesota History,* 28:20-36, March, 1947.

McMurtry, R. Gerald. "Republican Campaign Problems of 1860: Letter of N. B. Judd to Cassius M. Clay, Dated Aug. 14, 1860," *Lincoln Herald,* 48:43-44, February, 1946.

Millsap, Kenneth F. "The Election of 1860 in Iowa," *Iowa Journal of History,* 48:97-120, April, 1950.

Splitter, H. W. "Lincoln Rails in the California Presidential Campaign of 1860," *Pacific Historical Review*, 19:351-55, November, 1950.

Wiley, Earl W. "Ohio Pre-Convention Support for Lincoln in 1860," *Lincoln Herald*, 52:13-17, 39, June, 1950.

LINCOLN—FINANCES

Pratt, Harry E. *Personal Finances of Abraham Lincoln.* Springfield, Ill.: Abraham Lincoln Association, 1943.

LINCOLN'S POLITICAL PHILOSOPHY

BOOKS

Angle, Paul M., ed. *Created Equal? The Complete Lincoln-Douglas Debates of 1858.* Chicago: University of Chicago Press, 1958.

Gernon, Blaine B. *Lincoln in the Political Circus.* Chicago: Black Cat Press, 1936.

Hamilton, Charles G. *Lincoln and the Know-Nothing Movement.* Washington: Public Affairs Press, 1954.

Houser, Martin L. *Lincoln's Early Political Education.* Peoria, Ill.: L. O. Schriver, 1944.

Nevins, Allan. *The Statesmanship of the Civil War.* New York: Macmillan Co., 1953.

Packard, Roy D. *The Lincoln of the Thirtieth Congress.* Boston: Christopher Publishing House, 1950.

Riddle, Donald W. *Congressman Abraham Lincoln.* Urbana: University of Illinois Press, 1957.

―――. *Lincoln Runs for Congress.* New Brunswick, N. J.: Rutgers University Press, 1948.

ARTICLES

Ascher, L. W. "Lincoln's Administration and the New Almaden Scandal," *Pacific Historical Review*, 5:38-51, March, 1936.

Brooks, W. E. "Lincoln's Philosophy of History," *Christian Century*, 54:274-76, February 28, 1940.

Carter, J. D. "Abraham Lincoln and the California Patronage," *American Historical Review*, 48:495-506, April, 1943.

Current, Richard N. "Lincoln and Daniel Webster," *Journal of the Illinois State Historical Society*, 48:307-21, Autumn, 1955.

Farley, James A. "Lincoln the Politician," *Vital Speeches*, 11:313-15, March 1, 1945.

Miller, P. I. "Lincoln and the Governorship of Oregon," *Mississippi Valley Historical Review*, 23:391-94, December, 1936.

Stevenson, Adlai E. "Lincoln as a Political Leader," *Abraham Lincoln Quarterly*, 7:79-86, June, 1952.

"Torment of War: Lincoln's Philosophy," *Christian Century*, 60:159-61, February 10, 1943.

LINCOLN'S RELATION WITH THE CABINET AND CONGRESS

Baringer, William E. *A House Dividing.* Springfield, Ill.: Abraham Lincoln Association, 1945.

Bryson, L. "Lincoln in Power," *Political Science Quarterly*, 61:161-74, June, 1946.

Hacker, Louis M. "Lincoln and the Republicans," *American Mercury*, 62:370-75, March, 1946.

Hendrick, Burton J. *Lincoln's War Cabinet.* Boston: Little, Brown, 1946.

McLaughlin, A. C. "Lincoln, the Constitution and Democracy," *International Journal of Ethics*, 47:1-24, October, 1936.

McReynolds, Edwin C. "The Influence of the Cabinet during the American Civil War" (University of Oklahoma, *Abstract of Thesis*, 1:258-67, 1950).

Pratt, Harry E. "Simon Cameron's Fight for a Place in Lincoln's Cabinet," *Bulletin of the Abraham Lincoln Association*, 49:3-11, September, 1937.

Russ, William A. "The Struggle between President Lincoln and Congress over Disfranchisement of Rebels [1862-65]," *Susquehanna University Standard*, 3:221-43, March, 1948.

ERNEST M. ESPELIE

Abraham Lincoln, 1860-1960
Books and Pamphlets in the

Augustana College Library

"Furthermore, my son, be admonished: Of making many books there is no end."—Eccles. 12:12.

Of making Lincoln books there is no end. To paraphrase the Bible in introducing an unassuming bibliography of Lincolniana seems unnecessary when it is obvious to all that a new Lincoln title is listed in practically every issue of the Sunday New York *Times Book Review.* Yet such a paraphrase is fitting when one considers that the Bible was the youthful Lincoln's best teacher. Certainly he studied it more than any of the books he possessed as a boy—studied it for the disciplines it taught him, for the lessons in reading, spelling and rhetoric, and for the pure literary style of the King James version. For a boy who attended only backwoods schools in Kentucky and Indiana (and that for a total of less than twelve months) and possessed only a half dozen books (the Bible, *Pilgrim's Progress, Robinson Crusoe, Aesop's Fables,* Weems' *Life of Washington* and Weems' *Life of Gen. Francis Marion*) during those formative years, it is almost unbelievable that a midwestern college library should be listing its holdings of materials about him as something of continuing interest—and that 150 years after his birth!

But why should a college library of 100,000 volumes list its modest holdings when it has made no special effort to collect Lincolniana? Augustana College is this year celebrating her centennial—just one hundred years after Lincoln was elected President—and the thought is that her Lincolniana may well be representative of the average liberal arts college, and for that reason, of interest.

No attempt has been made in this bibliography of 265 titles to list the hundreds of articles in periodicals and newspapers, or the chapters in Civil War and political histories that relate to Lincoln and his administration. Many of these articles, were they analyzed, especially those in the Swedish immigrant newspaper *Hemlandet* (which undoubtedly affords a better answer to the Swedish immigrants' attitudes toward Lincoln in the 1855-1860 period than any other printed source) would be equally as significant as are the listed materials.

Authors of Swedish ancestry are well represented in this bibliography, outstanding, of course, being Carl Sandburg, to whom this collection of essays is dedicated. Swedish Lincoln scholars listed herein are Ahlberg (entry no. 190), Ander (121), Grip (28), Hokanson (37), Oakleaf, the Swedish equivalent being Eklöf (130-133, 152 and 168), Olson (134), Sandburg (91-94, 188, 217 and 228), Skarstedt (98) and Wikberg (112)—a total of twenty titles. It is noteworthy, too, that this bibliography contains fourteen titles which are contemporary with Lincoln, i.e., published during the years 1860-1866.

The method of presentation used in this list is to first give the general titles followed by the special subject categories, alphabetically arranged much as they are in the library card catalog. Thus one can immediately ascertain the books Augustana has treating of Lincoln's family, or his religion. Although a book may well cover two or three subjects, it is listed only under the most pertinent subject, thus permitting consecutive numbering of titles.

When one considers the many facets of Lincoln literature, such as the occasions and anniversaries which lend themselves to publications, it is understandable, from the first book about Lincoln in 1860 to those that will appear in 1960, that there is a veritable inundation of Lincoln books. This man who owned few books and wrote none has indeed inspired more books than any man of modern times.

AUGUSTANA LINCOLNIANA—GENERAL

ADDRESSES, ESSAYS, LECTURES, SERMONS

Choate, Joseph H. *The Career and Character of Abraham Lincoln.* An Address Delivered by Joseph H. Choate, Ambassador to Great Britain, November 13, 1900. Chicago: Chicago, Milwaukee & St. Paul Railway [1901?] 30 pp. ...125
Donald, David H. *Lincoln Reconsidered; Essays on the Civil War Era.* New York: Knopf, 1956. 200 pp. 126
Graebner, Norman A., ed. *The Enduring Lincoln; Lincoln Sesquicentennial Lectures at the University of Illinois.* Urbana: Univ. of Ill. Pr., 1959. 129 pp. 127
Iowa. University. Library. Bollinger Lincoln Foundation. *The Bollinger Lincoln Lectures.* Edited by Clyde C. Walton, Jr. [Iowa City] State Univ. of Iowa Libraries, 1953. 80 pp. 128
Kuhn, Isaac, ed. *Abraham Lincoln; a Vast Future.* Champaign, Ill.: J. Kuhn, Priv. Print., 1946. 50 pp. 129
Oakleaf, Joseph B. *Abraham Lincoln; His Friendship for Humanity and Sacrifice for Others.* An Address by J. B. Oakleaf Delivered at Augustana College, Rock Island, Ill., by invitation of the faculty, Feb. 12, 1909. Moline: Desaulniers, 1910. 45 pp. 130
————*Abraham Lincoln, Meade, Lee and Gettysburg.* Peoria: E. J. Jacob, 1929. 16 pp. 131
————*An Address on Abraham Lincoln.* Cedar Rapids: Lawrence Pr., 1925. 14 pp. 132
————*Hobbies;* an Address on the Collection of Lincoln Literature . . . Delivered February 12, 1913 . . . Rock Island: Augustana Book Concern, 1923. 14 pp. 133
Svenskhetens Berömelse. Tva Märkliga Tal Översatta från Engelskan. I. President Calvin Coolidges Tal om John Ericsson. II. Överdomare Harry Olsons Tal om Abraham Lincoln . . . Chicago: Sjöstrand [1926] 32 pp. 134

ANECDOTES, CARICATURES

Carpenter, Francis B. *Six Months at the White House with Abraham Lincoln.* New York: Hurd and Houghton, 1867. 359 pp. 135
McClure, Alexander K. *Lincoln's Yarns and Stories* . . . Philadelphia: J. C. Winston [19—] 416 pp. 136
McClure, James B. *Anecdotes of Abraham Lincoln, and Lincoln Stories.* Chicago: Rhodes & McClure, 1879. 188 pp. 137
Selby, Paul. *Lincoln's Life, Stories and Speeches.* Chicago: Thompson & Thomas, c1902. 469 pp. 138
Shaw, Albert. *Abraham Lincoln* . . . [a cartoon history] New York: Review of Reviews, 1929. 2 vols. 139
Wilson, Rufus R. *Lincoln in Caricature* . . . New York: Horizon Press, 1953. 327 pp. 140

ANNIVERSARIES, MEMORIAL SERVICES

Bancroft, George. *Memorial Address on the Life and Character of Abraham Lincoln, Delivered, at the Request of Both Houses of The Congress of America, before Them, in the House of Representatives at Washington, on the 12th of February, 1866.* Washington: Gov't Print. Off., 1866. 69 pp. 141
Affixed to flyleaf is a Lincoln photograph signed: "Abraham."

144

AS A LAWYER

ASSASSINATION

Mudd, Samuel A. *The Life of Dr. Samuel A. Mudd; Containing His Letters from Fort Jefferson, Dry Tortugas Island, Where He Was Imprisoned Four Years for Alleged Complicity in the Assassination of Abraham Lincoln* . . . Marietta, Ga.: Continental Book Co., 1955. 363 pp. 160
First Published, 1906, by Neale Pub. Co., New York.

BIBLIOGRAPHY

DRAMA

FAMILY

148

PORTRAITS

RELIGION

LINCOLN-DOUGLAS DEBATES

ADDENDA

151

Contributors

O. Fritiof Ander is a professor of history at Augustana College. His works include *T. N. Hasselquist, the Career and Influence of a Swedish-American Clergyman, Educator, and Journalist* (1931), *The Cultural Heritage of the Swedish Immigrant* (1956), and *The Building of Modern Sweden* (1958). He edited the *John H. Hauberg Historical Essays* (1954) and was co-editor of *The American Origins of the Augustana Synod* (1942). He has prepared a number of bibliographies and numerous articles chiefly in the field of immigration. He was one of the founders of the *Junior Historian of Illinois* and the *American Heritage*.

Ernest Espelie had been librarian and professor at the U. S. Coast Guard Academy, New London, Conn., for twenty years when he succeeded Lucien W. White as librarian of the Denkmann Memorial Library, Augustana College. He is editor of the *Augustana College Library Publications* and *Occasional Papers*. The latter was begun by White and includes contributions by well-known historians. Edgar L. Erickson wrote *One Hundred Years of British Colonial Policy* (1958) while Louis Gottschalk contributed *The United States and Lafayette: Les Etats-Unis et Lafayette* (1958). The *Occasional Papers* for 1960, edited by Espelie, consist of a series of centennial lectures, one of which is Glen T. Seaborg's *Science and Liberal Education in the Space Age*.

Norman A. Graebner is professor of history at the University of Illinois. His books include *Empire on the Pacific* (1955), *The New Isolationism* (1956) and *The Enduring Lincoln* (1959) which he edited. His special field of interest is American politics and foreign policy. He delivered the Commonwealth Fund Lectures at the University of London in January and February of 1958 on "The Revolution in American Politics, 1837-1877." He is contributing editor of *Current History* and associate editor of *World Affairs Quarterly*. His course in American diplomacy was broadcast from the classroom during the academic year of 1958-1959 and during the past year he has had a weekly program entitled "Background of the News" over WBBM-CBS, Chicago. Graebner has authored numerous articles.

153

Ralph J. Roske is associate professor of history at Humboldt State College. He is the co-author of *Lincoln's Commando* (1957). Roske has also authored several articles including "Seven Martyrs?" which appeared in the *American Historical Review* of January of 1959. He is currently at work on a definitive biography of Lyman Trumbull.

Robert M. Sutton is associate professor of history as well as associate dean of the Graduate College at the University of Illinois and a director of Illinois State Historical Society. Dr. Sutton's writing has been largely centered on the development of midwestern transportation with his major work being on the role of the Illinois Central Railroad during the Civil War. He has published articles and reviews in a number of the leading historical journals of the country.

Clyde C. Walton is Illinois state historian, executive director of the Illinois State Historical Society and secretary of the Illinois Lincoln Sesquicentennial Commission. He is also the editor of the *Journal of the Illinois State Historical Society* and of the quarterly magazine *Civil War History* which he founded. The latter is published by the State University of Iowa. He edited *Bollinger Lincoln Lectures* and *25 Books in the Bollinger Lincoln Collection* for the University of Iowa. He is also the author of a number of articles.

T. Harry Williams is Boyd professor of history at Louisiana State University. He is author of *Lincoln and the Radicals* (1941), *Lincoln and His Generals* (1952), and *P. G. T. Beauregard* (1955). He collaborated with Richard N. Current and Frank Freidel in preparing the two volume college text *A History of the United States* (1959). He is editor of *Selected Writings and Speeches of Abraham Lincoln* (1943), *With Beauregard in Mexico* (1956), and *Abraham Lincoln—Selected Speeches and Letters* (1957). Williams, a past president of Southern Historical Association, is one of the foremost students of Lincoln today.

INDEX

Abraham Lincoln Association, 101
Abolitionists, 16
Adams, Charles Francis, 87, 88
Adams, Henry, 1, 2
Aesop's Fables, 137
Ahlberg, Albert, 138
Alabama, 46
Albany, 46
Almighty, 22
Alton, Illinois, 67
Alton and Sangamon Railroad, 47, 48
America, Americans for, 5; economy, 27; institutions, 86; liberties, 12; loyalty to, 3; mission, 86-87; nation, 27; people, 33; resources, 1, 12; society, 93; struggle in, 90-91; mentioned, 4, 9, 21
"America fever," 3
American, affairs, 89; commitment, 92; culture, 25; democracy, 86; dilemma, 21-22; diplomacy, 83-98; flag, 3, 19; history, 103, 104; idealism, 84; influences on immigrants, 5; institutions, 84; minister in St. Petersburg, 90; nation, 26; people of 1850, 37; politics, 10; power, 9; religious tolerance, 4; railroads, 41, 45; scene (1860), 38; shores, 84; soil, 95; struggle, 90
American Historical Review, 99
American Home Missionary Society, 3
Americanization, 1-3, 5, 21
American Lutherans, 3-4
American Republic, 85
American Union, 87
Americans, distinguished, 84; justice for, 96
Americans Interpret Their Civil War, 25
Ander, O. Fritiof, 138
Andover, Illinois, 19
Andreen, O. C. T., 3, 21
Antebellum leaders, 29
Anti-Nebraska Democrats, 66, 68
Aristotle, 21
Arkansas, 79
Arnold, Isaac N., 76
Atlantic, 29
Atlantic and Mississippi Railroad, 47

Atlantic Monthly, 30
Atlantic seaboard states, 3
Augustana College and Theological Seminary, beginnings, 1, 2, 8, 16, 20-21; books and pamphlets, 137-151
Augustana Lutheran Church, origins 1-4 (see also Swedish Lutherans and Swedish immigrants)
Austria, 91
Austrian Hapsburg, 85
Bacon Academy, 62
Baker, Edward D., 63, 74
Baltimore Convention, 78
Baptists, 3
Barlow, S. L. M., 101
Battle-Hymn of the Republic, 22
Beard, Charles A., 25-26
Becker, Carl, 37
Beecher, Edward, 13
Belleville, Illinois, 62
Bible, 137
Bishop Hill, Illinois, 19
Bissell, William Henry, 54
Blegen, Theodore C., 11
Bloomington, Illinois, 13, 42, 49
Boston, Massachusetts, 46
Brayman, Mason, 48, 50-51
Breckinridge, John C., 18, 20
Breese, Sidney, 45, 63
British, 87
Brown, Charles Leroy, 54, 55
Brown, C. W., 13
Brown, George T., 78
Browning, Orville H., 63
Buchanan, James, 12, 13, 69-70
Cairo, Illinois, 42, 60
Cameron, Simon, 74
Campaign (1858), 70-71; (1860), 72-73; (1862), 77 (see also Elections)
Campbell, Thompson, 64
Carey, Henry, 17
Carlin, Thomas, 63, 64
Carlsson, Erland, 3, 15
Carthage, Illinois, 59
Cass, Lewis, 84
Catholics, 16
Channing, Edward, 25
Champaign County, 48, 50

155

Republican Radicals, 94 (see also Radicals)
Republicans, Congress (1864-65), 79; noisy group, 68; split, 72; success, 69; support of Lincoln, 70; Trumbull, 76-77; mentioned, 21
Revisionists, 26-27
Reynolds, John, 62, 63
Reynolds, W. M., 6
Rhodes, James Ford, 25
Richardson, William A., 63
Richmond, Virginia, 88
Robinson, Solon, 44
Robinson Crusoe, 137
Rock Island, Illinois, 57
Roman Catholic Church, 10
Russia, 91
Russian Czar, 91

St. Louis Missouri, 32, 56, 57
St. Louis *Republican,* 57
"Sand Bar Case," 55
Sandburg, Carl, 101, 137
Sangamon Circuit Court, 64
Sangamon County, 43
Sangamon River, 42
San Francisco, California, 32
Scandinavian, newspapers, 11; professorship, 3-4, 5, 8, 14
Scandinavians, 8-9, 14, 16
Schlesinger, A. M., Jr., 28
Schurz, Carl, 16, 18
"Second American Revolution," 26
Sectionalistic issues, 29-39
Senate (U. S.), 30-31, 45, 68, 72, 73, 79
Senate Judiciary Committee, 79
Seward, William H., antebellum leader, 29; Civil War, 28; diplomacy, 87-93; favored, 15; politics as Secretary of State, 87-93; Trumbull, 72; mentioned 19, 74, 75
Sherman, John, 29
Shields, James, 63, 67, 71
Skarstedt, Ernst, 138
Skenlund, A. A., 19
Slavery (issue of), 33-35, 38, 39 (see Campaigns and Elections)
Smith, Robert, 65
South, citizens of, 95; destruction of, 94; economic system, 29-31; expansion of slavery, 33; Kansas-Nebraska Act, 66; political power, 30-31; pressure upon, 26; railroad mileage, 60; secession, 73; self-determination, 90; social system, 30; support of, 46; Trumbull, 73; Union, 94; mentioned, 21, 38, 39
South Carolina, 29, 73
Southerners, 30-31, 34, 35, 66
"Southern Vindicators," 26
Spain, 92
Sprague, Kate Chase, 77-78
Springer, Francis, 5
Springfield, Illinois, home of Illinois State University, 4-9; state capitol, 43, 69; mentioned, 4, 5, 8, 13, 14, 41, 59, 64, 65, 73, 85
"Springfield Clique," 65
State Republican Convention, 13 (see also Illinois State Republican Convention and Republican, conventions)
Stolbrand, C. J., 18
Stuart, John T., 4-5, 52
Sumner, Charles, 79, 80
Sundell, Charles J., 18
Superior Court of Georgia, 62
Supreme Court of Illinois, 36, 50, 54-55, 72
Supreme Court of Ohio, 53
Sweden, Established Church of, 3; universities, 3; mentioned, 21
Swedes, 10, 14, 17-20
Swedish-American newspaper, 21 (see names of newspapers)
Swedish, authors, 138; churches, 18; colonists, 5; immigrants, 1-3, 12; flags, 19; Lincoln, 9, 138; Lutherans, 12, 18; Republican clubs, 19
Swensson, Jonas, 3
Synod of Northern Illinois, 3, 4, 6, 16

Taney, Roger B., 36
Terre Haute and Alton Railroad, 48, 56
Thirtieth Congress, 45
Thomas, Benjamin P., 100, 101
Thirteenth Amendment, 78-79
Thoreau, Henry, 12
Thomas, J. B., 50
Times (London), 90
Todd, Mary, 63, 64-65
Tonica and Petersburg Railroad, 48
Trumbull, Julia Jayne, 77
Trumbull, Lyman, birth, 61; campaign of 1860, 72-73; career, 61-81; Democratic party, 62; educator, 61-62; Lincoln, 73-81; public speaker, 61; reconstruction, 78-80; Republican, 68-81; schoolteacher, 62; Secretary of State (Illinois), 64; mentioned, 9, 65

160

Uncle Tom's Cabin, 13
Union (U. S.), 21, 31, 78, 83, 86-87, 89, 91, 93-94, 96, 98
Union party, 78
United States, government, 90; involvement, 91-92; nationalism, 32; presidency of, 1; railroads of, 60; Senate, 14, 41, 84; world power, 25; mentioned, 85, 86
United States Supreme Court, 58, 69
Utilior Society (Illinois State University), 7-8
Van Buren, Martin, 62
Vandalia, Illinois, 43
Vermont, Illinois, 59
Victoria, Illinois, 19
Virginia, 31
Wabash Railroad, 48
Wabash River, 42
Walnut Grove, Illinois, 19
Washington, D. C., 73
Washington, George, 83, 84, 85
Washington, H. A., 31
Wautauga, Illinois, 18
Webb, Edwin B., 65

Webber, T. R., 50
Webster, Daniel, 84
Webster (Dictionary), 103
Weem's *Life of Gen. Francis Marion; Life of Washington,* 137
Wentworth, "Long John," 71-72
West, railroads, 46
Western World, 31
Whig party, aloofness, 9; cause of, 62; death, 11; dissolution, 68-69; Illinois, 47, 67; internal improvements, 44; program, 29; tariff, 16; wing of, 73; mentioned, 16, 62, 65, 67, 68, 69
White House, 75, 103
Whitman, Walt., 22
Whitney, Henry C., 48
Wide Awake, 18, 19
"Wigwam," 55
Wilson, Woodrow, 25
Wisconsin, 16
World War I, 25
World War II, 27
Yale, 61, 62
Yankee, 62
Yates, Richard, 60, 63

WITHDRAWN